SEX AND RUSSIAN SOCIETY

SEX AND RUSSIAN SOCIETY

Edited by
Igor Kon and **James Riordan**

Indiana University Press
BLOOMINGTON AND INDIANAPOLIS

First published in 1993 in the United States by
Indiana University Press
601 North Morton Street, Bloomington, IN

Copyright © 1993 by Igor Kon and James Riordan

Introduction copyright © 1993 James Riordan

Manufactured in the United States of America

Library of Congress Cataloging-in-Publication Data

Sex and Russian society / Igor Kon and James Riordan, editors.
p.   cm.
Includes bibliographical references (p.   ) and index.
ISBN 0–253–33200–1 (cloth), — ISBN 0–253–33201–X (pbk.)
1. Sex customs—Soviet Union.
2. Sex customs—Russia (Federation)
3. Communism and sex—Soviet Union.
4. Soviet Union—Moral conditions.   5. Russia
(Federation)—Moral conditions.   I. Kon,
Igor ' Semenovich.   II. Riordan, James.   date
HQ18.S65S46   1993
306.7'0947—dc20   92–33636

1 2 3 4 5   97 96 95 94 93

Contents

Contributors

Igor Kon, Member of the Academy of Pedagogical Sciences, is author of over 30 books, including such seminal monographs as *Adolescent Psychology* (1979) which sold some 1.5 million copies and was the first book of its kind in the USSR for 60 years. His *Introduction to Sexology* (1988) was banned for ten years and came out in Russian only in 1988 (though it had circulated widely in samizdat). He founded his own journal, *Eros*, in 1991 and has campaigned prominently for the decriminalisation of homosexuality. As a tribute to his studies of young people and sexuality, the Kinsey Institute dedicated to him its *Adolescence and Puberty* (1990).

Academician Kon's two chapters in this work present a historical overview of sexuality, and of the status of gays and lesbians, in Russian and Soviet society.

James Riordan, Professor of Russian Studies at the University of Surrey in the UK, is author of over 20 books on the Soviet Union and Eastern Europe, including the seminal *Sport in Soviet Society* (1977) and *Sport, Politics and Communism* (1991). His latest works include *Soviet Education: the Gifted and the Handicapped* (1988), *Soviet Youth Culture* (1989), *Dear Comrade Editor* (with Sue Bridger, 1991) and *Soviet Social Reality in the Mirror of Glasnost* (1992). He is a Fellow of the Royal Society for the Arts and Doctor honoris causa of Grenoble Stendhal University.

Professor Riordan has provided the translations of the five Russian chapters below, and undertaken the editing of the entire work. He has also written the introduction for Western readers to the sexual culture of Russian and Soviet society, in which he suggests some practical assistance that the West can give.

Larissa Remennick is a social scientist studying epidemiology and reproductive health. She received her doctorate from the Moscow

Institute of Sociology for her dissertation on 'Reproductive Patterns and Female Cancer Risks in the USSR'. Throughout her work Dr Remennick has placed much emphasis on the problem of high rates of induced abortion and the need for a modern family planning service in the former Soviet Union. Until recently she worked at the Cancer Research Centre attached to the USSR Academy of Medical Sciences in Moscow. She is now employed at the Department of Epidemiology, the Chaim Sheba Medical Centre, Tel-Hashomer, Israel.

In her chapter, Dr Remennick provides a wealth of research data on patterns of birth control in various parts of the old USSR, showing the high cost paid by women and society for the long reliance on abortion, the lack of condoms and other means of birth control.

Lynne Attwood, one of the most authoritative Western writers on Soviet women, is author of *The New Soviet Man and Women: Sex Role Socialization in the USSR* (1990) and editor of *Red Women on the Silver Screen*. Having received her doctorate at the Centre for Russian and East European Studies, University of Birmingham (UK), she has held lecturing posts at the University of Texas and Humberside Polytechnic; she is currently lecturer in Soviet Studies at the University of Manchester.

In her contribution to this book, Dr Attwood details the development of sex and pornography in Soviet and Russian film in recent years: from the virtually sexless films before 1985 to a situation where, as she writes, the sex act became a virtually obligatory feature of films in the era of perestroika.

Elizabeth Waters lived and worked for a number of years in Moscow, and is married to a Russian citizen. She now teaches Russian and Soviet History at the Australian National University. She has written widely on women, the family and social problems in the contemporary USSR and Russia, and in the post-revolutionary period. Her *Women in a Bolshevik World: Work, Marriage and Motherhood in Urban Russia, 1917–1928* was published in 1992. She is currently working on *Gender and Soviet Society* and on a social history of prostitution in the USSR during the 1920s and early 1930s.

Here Dr Waters traces the evolution of various forms of beauty contests that began to be held from 1988 up and down the Soviet Union, and discusses the dilemmas they posed for a society in transition from its puritanical past to a market-driven future.

Sergei Golod wrote his doctoral dissertation in the late 1960s, under Igor Kon's supervision, on sexual behaviour and adolescent sex attitudes. When he presented it in 1969, first the Leningrad Party, then the Komsomol accused him of 'ideological diversion against Soviet youth'. He therefore had to write a completely new dissertation on 'working women' (*not* in the Western sense of the term) who, of course, had no time for sex . . . Dr Golod has conducted numerous surveys on the sexual behaviour of young people and published a number of monographs on sexual mores of the 1920s. He is currently working at the St Petersburg branch of the Institute of Sociology.

In his chapter in the present work, he describes the remarkable changes that have taken place in young people's sexual behaviour and attitudes in recent years.

Lev Shcheglov is a medical doctor residing in St Petersburg. He has written a number of works on the medical aspects of the relatively new discipline (in Russia and the other former Soviet republics) of sexology. Here he describes the history and current status of medical sexology or 'sexopathology', the difficult path it has had to traverse and the continuing hostility to it from much of the medical establishment and the authorities.

Introduction

JAMES RIORDAN

Writing a book on sex in any society risks attracting accusations of sensationalism, exaggeration, voyeurism – the more so if one is on the outside looking in, if scholarly material is at a premium and ignorance is abundant. And when that society is the old Soviet Union and its successor Commonwealth, with its longstanding official puritanism and hypocrisy, yet seductive allure for Westerners, the pitfalls are deep and numerous.

Our team of four Russian and three Western scholars, four men and three women, has set out to make a serious study of sexuality in Russian society. It is a subject oddly overlooked or avoided by most Western students of the erstwhile USSR; yet it is surely no less salient a facet of human behaviour than, say, education, labour relations or even religion. It was none other than the religious philosopher Nikolai Berdyaev who said that 'all relationships took shape and developed through sex, since sex is, after all, a matter of life and death.'[1]

If ignorance of sex in Russian society is a fact of life for many Westerners, it has been a matter of death each year for many Russians. For example, as many as 2,020 women died between 1986 and 1988 as a result of having abortions (in the US, with a comparable female population, the figure was 27 between 1983 and 1985),[2] and it is estimated that AIDS will have claimed some 6,000 victims by 1995.[3] Then there are the unknown number of suicides by sexual minorities in a society where gay love has certainly dared not speak its name, and the broken marriages caused by unhappy sex lives based on ignorance.

Lack of information about sex or, rather, lack of a sex culture, together with suppression of anything that deviates from straightforward marital sex in the bedroom, was a feature of Soviet society

1

from the 1930s. Yet, as Igor Kon explains (see Chapter 1 below), its
roots go deep into Russian history. The medieval Russian Orthodox
Church was much more restrictive than the church in Western
Europe in regard to representations of the human body, as any
comparison of Russian icons and Renaissance art reveals. But it was
not only the church that enforced puritanism in sexual matters. In the
nineteenth century, the emergent Russian erotic art and literature
had to contend with both church and state, and the radical intelligentsia – writers like Belinsky and Chernyshevsky – which tried to
subjugate individual, particularly sensual, values to sociopolitical
themes. These repressive intellectual attitudes delayed the development of a more tolerant attitude to sex and made all sexual imagery
appear low and salacious, thereby providing moral justification for
the later Stalinist policies.

It is true that the Russian Revolution of October 1917 opened up
discussion of sexuality, including 'free love', and introduced the most
liberal legislation in the world at the time (for instance, the decriminalisation of homosexuality and the legalisation of abortion, which
became free and available on demand). The 'sexual revolution',
however, did not extend beyond a relatively small group of 'liberated'
intellectuals and young workers in European centres. Nor did it last.
In the early 1930s the situation began rapidly to deteriorate. Sex
surveys were banned, together with sociology and social psychology
as academic disciplines. Command-administrative control of sexual
affairs replaced social-moral regulation. In 1934 the authorities
recriminalised male homosexuality (which became punishable by up
to eight years' deprivation of freedom); abortions were banned two
years later (the ban lasted till 1955); all forms of erotic art were
censured; and schools ceased to teach sex education. The public was
left sexually illiterate and society officially became sexless, even
genderless.

Current revulsion with the old communist regime partly stems from
a realisation that the atmosphere of moral rectitude that it created
was cynically exploited for ideological ends. George Orwell put it
aptly in his novel *1984* in summing up the repression of sex:

> It was not merely that the sex instinct created a world of its own
> that was outside the Party's control and which therefore had to be
> destroyed if possible. What was more important was that sexual
> privation induced hysteria, which was desirable because it could be
> transformed into war-fever and leader-worship.[4]

Not that the privileged and powerful were sexually deprived. We now know that while publicly haranguing others about morality, some Party bosses and apparatchiks lived lives of debauchery. Stalin's police chief, Lavrenty Beria, is known to have been what the dramatist Eduard Radzinsky calls 'a dissolute sadist'.[5] Private 'blue film' showings, secret Party brothels and massage parlours existed for the elite, with young girls recruited or forced into service from Komsomol colleges and, in one scandalous instance, from a home for young blind girls in a Central Asian republic.[6] Even in Khrushchov's time, in the 1950s, a Minister of Culture (Alexandrov) was on the board of directors of a clandestine brothel and recruited female students from theatrical schools to 'reenact scenes straight out of the Satiricon'.[7] Such moral hypocrisy on the part of some communist leaders and functionaries has done irreparable damage to the political cause they affected to espouse and the moral structures they erected.

From the late 1970s, the moral climate slowly changed. When Igor Kon published his *Adolescent Psychology* in 1979, it was the first book of its kind for 60 years. His pioneering *Introduction to Sexology* had a ten-year ban lifted only in 1988. But the long years of repression have taken their toll. The 'sexual revolution' is today taking place in an environment of social, political, economic and moral crisis and among a sexually ignorant, conservative and fundamentally sexist population, especially in the countryside, Central Asia and the Caucasus. This 'revolution' has induced a state of shock and moral panic in many people. When the Moscow youth paper *Moskovsky komsomolets* published a mildly educational article on childbirth in 1990, it received the following outraged letter from a woman in the provinces:

You are depraved and disgusting! To whom are you explaining where children come from? People old enough already know or can find out for themselves. But 3–5, even 14–15 year olds don't need to know . . . We knew nothing about 'sex' or 'erotica' before, but we still produced healthy children. We knew how to do it without lessons from you. We had real love, a sense of duty, love for our mothers, our country, patriotism, and so on. What sort of children are you bringing up now? Look what your democracy brings! What we need is a Stalin or a merciless God! May your tongue, hands and organs drop off. Go to hell. You're all scum, swine, bastards.

Krylova (Dmitrov)[8]

To many individuals confronted for the first time with a frank discussion on an intimate theme, sex is bound to appear ugly and uncivilised; they look back with nostalgia to a time when the guidelines were unambiguous, when the strong master did the thinking for them. The new thinking, including on sex, presents a threat to firm traditions, law and order, and security. Small wonder the writer of the above letter looks to representatives of totalitarianism and religion, both traditionally arch foes of sexual free thinking. Such conservatism, especially in the older generation and Islamic areas of the Commonwealth, is a warning that the public cannot be bludgeoned into accepting a more enlightened sexual culture. Those people impatient with the 'old-fashioned' views of others must consider national and religious diversities, and must beware of offending national sentiments and traditions – however noble the cause. It should also caution the often well-meaning Western 'missionaries' (such as gay activists) that conditions which have evolved over many years in the West cannot be reproduced in the onetime USSR overnight).

Some Consequences of Long Neglect and Repression

Many of the consequences of the years of neglect and repression are dealt with in this book. They may be summarised as follows.[9]

Extreme Ignorance of Sex as a Result of a Lack of Sex Education at School and Home

In as much as children and young people have received no systematic sex education, they have had to cull information largely from dog-eared, pre-revolutionary books or from hearsay. In a public opinion poll conducted in Russia in February 1991, as many as 87 per cent of the respondents said that their parents had never spoken to them about sex.[10] So if little sex information is available at home, what is given in schools? Although all schoolchilden formally have had (since 1983) twelve hours a year of 'hygiene and sex education' for 15 year-olds, and 34 hours a year of 'ethics and psychology of family life' for 16–17 year-olds, in practice schools provide, as Lev Shcheglov says, 'no sex education at all' (see p. 158 below). Even students at medical and educational colleges receive no systematic sexual information. And this despite the fact that the above-mentioned poll showed that

60 per cent of the respondents favoured sex education in school from the age of 11.[11]

Backwardness and lack of sexual satisfaction make people unhappy, cause neuroses, intolerance and aggression. On the other hand, the rebellion by young people against the old 'morality' has resulted in considerable sexual promiscuity and lack of scruple in choosing a partner. This encourages not only moral dissoluteness but the spread of venereal disease which, in recent years, has merged with the AIDS epidemic. In 1990 there were as many as 14,000 VD sufferers among children (up to 16 years of age) registered each year, two thirds of whom were young girls.[12] The following year, 1,500 young people under 18 had syphilis and 68,000 had gonorrhoea.[13] No moralising can replace proper medical education.

A Low Contraceptive Culture and High Abortion Rate

After the 1917 Revolution, Russia had the most progressive abortion laws in the world: terminations were performed in state hospitals free of charge, at a woman's request. By 1936 Stalin decided that the country needed a larger workforce and army, so he introduced a law banning abortions save in exceptional medical circumstances. Owing to the mounting number of complications from self-induced or backstreet abortions, and to the very modest rise in birth rates achieved, the ban was lifted in 1955 (after Stalin's death). Since then induced abortion (IA) has been the principal means of birth control in the old USSR. The contraceptive revolution in the West heralded by the advent of the Pill in the mid-1960s never reached the Soviet Union, and IA inevitably became the main instrument of the postwar fertility decline (see Chapter 2 below).

One reason for the high abortion rate is the shortage of contraceptives: in the mid-1980s the supply of all forms of contraceptives from retail outlets comprised roughly a fifth of the estimated need; in 1989 the production of condoms amounted to three a year for every adult male.[14] Thus many women have had no alternative but to rely on IA in cases of unwanted pregnancies.

The major cause of the high abortion rate, however, is inadequate information and incompetence, resulting in the highest abortion rate in the world (most women have on average between two or three abortions), with all the medical and moral implications that 10 million abortions a year bring. In 1990 the USSR had 98.4 abortions per

1,000 women aged 15–49 and 127 abortions per 1,000 children born; this compares with 5.3 and 14.3 in Germany, and 8.7 and 16.2 in the US, respectively.[15]

A Sharp Rise in Sexual Violence and Child Abuse

As in the West, the increase in reported sexual violence is partly the result of more efficient and reliable public accounting. But the statistics also reveal a steep rise owing to the profound crisis in society and the breakdown in morality among the younger generation; one consequence of this is higher juvenile delinquency, general crime and violence.

The rapid growth in sexual violence in recent years is a very worrying phenomenon. In 1988 the official figure for rape and sexual assault was 17,658, yet by 1989 it had risen to 21,873.[16] These incidents primarily involved assaults on the streets committed by young people. What is more, according to the Ministry for Internal Affairs, in 1988 every fourth person convicted of rape was a minor, while 86.7 per cent convicted of rape were aged under 30. For the most part, these youths were school and technical college students. Other doleful statistics are that every fourth rape is a group or gang rape, and every fifth reform-school boy is a rapist.[17]

A root cause of sexual violence would appear to lie in the traditional stereotype of strong and aggressive masculinity. In a survey of Moscow young women in 1991, four fifths complained of sexual harassment on the street or at work, and a quarter said that their husbands or partners, especially when drunk, forced them to have sex against their will.[18]

It has to be said, in passing, that no professional psychological assistance exists either for rape victims or for sex offenders. Meanwhile, much of the media and conservative public opinion directly link the rise in sexual violence with democracy, the liberalisation of sexual mores and the baneful Western influence upon young people. It is significant that one of the first acts of the leaders of the attempted coup of 19–22 August 1991 was to declare 'war on the youth-inspired cult of sex and rock music'.[19]

Inadequate Measures to Combat AIDS

Initially, in 1986, when the first person with AIDS was registered in the USSR (a foreigner), the disease was discreetly reported as a

Western problem, with overtones of retribution for bourgeois depravity, and accusations against the CIA for unleashing the virus through an experiment gone wrong. Valuable time was lost in developing a campaign to protect the population. Still today, the media remain virtually inactive on the AIDS menace; it is only specialist periodicals like *SPID-info* (with a 2 million print run), the gay papers *Tema* and *RISK*, and the popular weekly magazine *Ogonyok* that report on AIDS. Even under Gorbachov the Soviet government refused to recognise the 1988 London Declaration of the World Health Organisation on AIDS information.

In March 1991 the results of testing 90 million people recorded 619 cases of HIV, including 267 children – a sevenfold increase in just three years. Of that number 54 had full-blown AIDS, of whom 34 were children. In the following 18 months 33 died, including 20 children.[20] The children had caught the infection in hospitals through staff using either infected blood or dirty equipment.

No adequate production or imports of disposable syringes and needles exist, and 'safer' sex is hampered by the lack and unreliability of contraceptives. Further, by the early 1990s no professional psychologists or sociologists had been included in the official AIDS-prevention programmes, as a result of which naive and primitive moralising often took the place of sober scientific analysis.

The situation is complicated further by the rapid rise in prostitution with the breakdown in morality and the transition to market relations (including the selling of sex – 'as they do in free Western societies'). In addition to the older prostitutes (those aged 17–25), however, society faces a worrying increase in the number of young girls selling their bodies for a paltry sum, often at railway stations. These 'railway children' are normally between 11 and 16 years of age and, in the crisis-ridden country, find prostitution the quickest and 'easiest' way to earn money. Inevitably, since very few of the girls employ any form of contraception, the swift increase in prostitution is adding to the rising incidence of sexually transmitted disease, including AIDS.

The Tragic Status of Sexual Minorities

As Igor Kon shows (see Chapter 4 below), sexual minorities are the most tragic victims of the lack of a sexual culture and pervasive ignorance. In spite of glasnost, male homosexuality was still a serious criminal offence in the early 1990s, and gays and lesbians were systematically discriminated against, victimised and humiliated. An idea of the generally prevailing homophobia may be gathered from a survey conducted by the (then) USSR Public Opinion Research Centre in late 1989. It found that 33 per cent of the respondents said that gays ought to be shot, another 30 per cent said they should be imprisoned, 30 per cent favoured forcible medical treatment, and only 6 per cent advocated 'assistance' of some sort and said that gays should be left alone. In Central Asia, those advocating capital punishment exceeded 85 per cent of all respondents.[21]

Mass homophobic sentiments have been encouraged by public statements from authoritative medical and police figures – like the President of the Academy of Medical Sciences, Valentin Pokrovsky (see Chapter 4, p. 95, below), and police official Victor Kachanov, both of whom bitterly and emotively opposed decriminalisation of homosexuality, the latter on the grounds that 'homosexuals pervert children, damaging them irreparably . . . Homosexuals are persons with inborn or socially conditioned mental disorders, and a genetic disposition to such sexual perversions. Decriminalisation would lead to such people going unpunished'.[22] And that in the liberal mass-circulation *Argumenty i fakty* (although it did print a reply from Igor Kon in the next issue).[23]

Although they were unrecognised by Russian law until 1992, lesbians find life no easier than gay men. A young girl who is aware of her psychosexual difference from the norm has found it harder than a man to discover a close relationship. As Olga Zhuk, a founder of the first lesbian and gay group in St Petersburg (the Tchaikovsky Cultural Foundation) has put it, 'for lesbians there are no places to meet or make acquaintances'.[24] It is a comment on the stupidity of official attitudes that the authorities refused to register her lesbian organisation on the grounds that it contravened Article 121 of the penal code (which deals with 'sodomy').[25]

In early 1992, some parliaments in the now-independent states that made up the USSR debated new penal codes which would decriminalise homosexuality. In both Russia and the Ukraine, for example, the new draft law revokes the infamous Article 121, and reduces the age of sexual consent for all persons from 18 to 16. For the first time lesbianism came to be recognised in the draft legislation. However, homosexuals were concerned that in Russia the draft law applying to homosexual rape (Article 132) differed markedly from its non-gay counterpart, referring to 'gay male sex, lesbianism and the gratification of sexual lust in other perverted forms'. The parallel draft law, which applies to heterosexuals, simply refers to 'sexual relations'.[26] No one knows when the draft law will be put on the statute books.

A Torrent of Pornography

The weakening of censorship and control over sexually explicit material has stimulated the underground production and dissemination of third-rate pornographic and semi-pornographic publications, films and videos; the opening of sex shops;[27] the holding of nude 'striptease' contests;[28] and a proliferation of sex shows. Both Lynne Attwood and Elizabeth Waters (see Chapters 3 and 5 below) show in some detail the inroads that have been made through the film industry and beauty contests respectively. Particularly in regard to films, it is clear that the proliferation of images of sexual violence against women is hardly likely to further the cause of women's liberation or equality; nor is it likely to nurture a new morality and self-respect among both genders.

In April 1991 the USSR Supreme Soviet passed a resolution 'On Urgent Measures to Prevent the Propagation of Pornography, the Cult of Violence and Cruelty'; sadly, this contained nothing but repressive and restrictive measures, and was silent on the need for sex education and the development of a sexual culture, as recommended by eminent psychologists, sociologists and medical officials. Without a constructive input, the anti-pornography programme is likely to have the opposite effect than the one intended, as such bans have demonstrated in the West and Japan.

Glimmers of Hope for the Future

Despite the unpropitious social and economic situation in the country, and the lack of government support (although some of the new governments, particularly in the three Slav states – Russia, Belorussia and the Ukraine – have started to introduce family planning policies, involving sex education, and have decriminalised homosexuality), considerable progress has been made in recent years in sex research and education.

Sex research centres have been created and attached to medical training colleges, as well as to the Moscow Institute of Psychiatry. 'Sexopathology' is now acknowledged as an independent clinical subdiscipline (as Lev Shcheglov shows in Chapter 7 below). Several textbooks and manuals for specialists have been published. A course for medical students was in preparation in 1991 and medical-psychological clinics now exist in many cities.

A number of sex education centres for young people have opened, and some popular books for adolescents and the general public have appeared, including the French manual for children '*Encyclopédie de la vie sexuelle* – even though its publication provoked much outrage in the conservative press. Alex Comfort's *The Joy of Sex* was printed in 1991; and the first issue of the popular journal *Eros*, edited by Igor Kon, was published in October 1991 (the second and third issues were ready for publication in 1992). The monthly *Literaturnoye obozrenie* (*Literary Review*) devoted its entire November 1991 issue to 'the erotic tradition in Russian literature'.[29] The same year saw the publication of an eight-page periodical for women, *Gazeta dlya zhenshchin*, containing advice on sex, and the featuring of regular advice columns for teenagers and young married couples in a number of popular newspapers. For example, the Moscow daily *Moskovsky komsomolets* now has weekly columns on 'Teenager' and 'Klub molodoi semyi' ('Young Family Club').

Some research on gender and sexuality is now being undertaken. A small Centre for Gender Studies was set up in 1990 within the USSR Institute for Socioeconomic Population Studies; in 1991, question-naires on sexual behaviour and the sex attitudes of teenagers and university students were drawn up at Moscow's Institute of Socio-logy. Research into gender stereotypes and the anthropology of the body is in progress at the Institute of the Ethnography and Anthropo-logy. In May 1990 the Estonian History Institute played host to an international conference on sexual minorities (the first ever in the Soviet Union); and joint Estonian–Finnish–Russian research on sexual minorities is underway. Following that, gay organisations held their first conferences concurrently in Moscow and St Petersburg in mid-1991 and have forged strong international links.

In the absence of support for sex education from the authorities, the way forward is being shown by voluntary trusts and charities, such as the Family and Health Association (primarily concerned with family planning), the Association for Combating AIDS (publishing the journal *SPID-info*), the Health and Culture Association (promot-ing sex education), the *Ogonyok* Anti-AIDS Charity and the Asso-ciation for Combating Sexually Transmitted Diseases. The major objectives of such associations are to promote and coordinate sex education and research, interdisciplinary expertise on social, educational and medical projects, and international consultation.

An Appeal for Help

As in other fields of research and voluntary services, sexology in the former Soviet Union faces two paramount problems: a shortage of funds and, even more important, a lack of trained personnel and information. What is urgently needed at the present is the following:

(1) Major textbooks and periodicals on sex education. Individual sexologists and even academic libraries have no foreign currency with which to purchase such books and periodicals.
(2) Agreement from Western publishers to grant the copyright for Russian translations of sexological books with payment in roubles, so that the best, rather than the cheapest, books can be made available to the public.
(3) Free individual membership of international sexological societies, on the basis of careful professional assessment and selection, for leading scholars.
(4) Participation of Western scholars in professional seminars and courses in Russia, sponsored by such professional bodies as the Health and Culture Association.
(5) Some foreign scholarships for training and research made available to young researchers, including in clinical psychology and social work.
(6) Strong professional and moral support against homophobia and discrimination against sexual minorities, particularly when repressive measures are still being advocated by the health authorities as part of the anti-AIDS campaign.

Progress is slow, particularly in a climate of sexual ignorance and intolerance. But with the help of understanding individuals and organisations outside the new Commonwealth, much more can be achieved. Let my co-editor Igor Kon have the final word:

It is not easy to help us. You will have to be extremely patient. We are asking for everything for nothing (except our future). We are ofttimes unreliable and inefficient in communicating. We frequently promise more than we can deliver, and we overestimate your possibilities even more than our own. We are certainly not as

12   *Sex and Russian Society*

great as we once pretended; yet we are a very big country and one that cannot be ignored. In the final count, it has to be said that our problems are your problems too.

James Riordan   Portsmouth
                                            1992

References

1. N.A. Berdyaev, 'Metafizika pola i lyubvi', *Pereval*, 1907, no. 6, p. 16.
2. See Larissa Remennick, p. 60 below.
3. Aza Rakhmanova, quoted by Annie Feltham, 'AIDS in Leningrad', *British-Soviet Business*, July/August 1991, p. 17.
4. George Orwell, *1984* (London: 1967), p. 109.
5. Eduard Radzinsky, 'Prostitution: Green Light for Moral Hypocrisy', *Soviet Weekly*, 13 December 1990, p. 10.
6. Ibid.
7. Ibid.
8. 'Ili Stalin, ili Bog', *Moskovsky komsomolets*, 6 October 1990, p. 2.
9. Some of the material here is summarised from Igor Kon's plenary paper, 'Culture and Sexuality in the USSR', delivered at the Tenth World Congress of Sexology, Amsterdam, June 1991.
10. Vsesoyuzny tsentr po issledovaniyu obshchestvennovo mneniya, February 1991 (quoted with the kind permission of the All-Union Public Opinion Research Centre).
11. Ibid.
12. I. Konchakova and V. Romanenko, 'Yest li u nas budushcheye?', *Argumenty i fakty*, November 1991, no. 43, p. 4.
13. Ibid.
14. Alla Alova, 'Luchshe ne dumat?' *Ogonyok*, June 1989, no. 26, p. 28.
15. Nikolai Bakhroshin, 'Bednye vy nashi', *Sobesednik*, 1991, no. 22, p. 7.
16. N. Kofyrin, 'Kto ukhodit v neformaly . . .', *Argumenty i fakty*, 31 March–6 April 1990, no. 13, p. 1.
17. Natalia Airapetova, 'A shto kuyem?', *Sobesednik*, 12 March 1990, p. 3.
18. Adrien Geiges, 'Lyubov vne plana', *Argumenty i fakty*, March 1991, no. 12, p. 7.
19. See V. Gushchin and A. Petrov, 'O molodyozhi, sexe i nasilii', *Argumenty i fakty*, August 1991, no. 33, p. 8.
20. Rakhmanova in Feltham, 'AIDS in Leningrad', p. 18. Unofficial sources put the HIV figure at closer to 15,000 (see *Commersant*, 9 April 1992, p. 1).
21. Vsesoyuzny tsentr po issledovaniyu obshchestvennovo mneniya, November 1989 (quoted with the kind permission of the Centre).

22. Victor Kachanov, *Argumenty i fakty*, March 1990, no. 9, p. 8.
23. Igor Kon, 'Zakon i polovye prestupleniya', in ibid., March 1990, no. 12, p. 5.
24. Olga Zhuk (in conversation with Chris Woods), 'Stepping out of the Underground', *Gay Times*, February 1992, p. 22.
25. Ibid.
26. See *Gay Times*, January 1992, p. 14, and February 1992, p. 19.
27. F. Smirnov, 'Dozhili!', *Meditsinskaya gazeta*, 13 March 1992, no. 20, p. 2. The initiators of the opening of the first 'salon' named 'Intime' were the Health and Culture Association and the Medicine and Reproduction Centre. The multinational sex chain EREX supplies the products.
28. See 'V.D.', 'Devushki vsekh stran, razdevaites!' ('Girls of the world, undress!'), *Moskovsky komsomolets*', 10 December 1991, p. 3. Such contests are not confined to women. The gay magazine *Tema* in mid-1991 advertised a 'longest penis' contest (*Tema*, no. 5, 1991, p. 13).
29. *Literaturnoye obozrenie*, 1991, no. 11. The bulk of the 26 contributions was from emigré writers – an indication of the difficulty of obtaining material within the country.

1

Sexuality and Culture

IGOR KON

Sex, eroticism and sex education are currently acute social and political issues in Russia. They are argued about in newspapers and on television; they are debated during election campaigns and parliamentary sessions. Even the Western press casts an eye in their direction. Unfortunately, the bulk of coverage is superficial in the extreme and replete with errors; sensationalism frequently hampers an understanding of reality.*

For many decades Soviet society hypocritically portrayed itself as utterly asexual, even sexless; it eventually even convinced itself of such drivel. What then is taking place now? Is it a belated sexual revolution like that of the 1960s in the West? Or the crumbling of traditional pillars of Russian life? Or, simply, has the arcane become the mundane? Have Soviet people, their ideological bonds sundered, become as human as, and more or less identical to, their contemporaries elsewhere? To answer those questions we must delve into the Russian past.

Was there Sex in Ancient Rus?

If we are to believe the apologists for Great Russian chauvinism, there was *no* sex, nothing erotic at any time in 'holy Rus'. But 'holy

---

* The book by Mark Popovsky, *Tretiy lishny. On, ona i sovetsky rezhim* (London: Overseas Publications Interchange, 1985) contains substantial documentary material, including historical, on various aspects of Soviet sexual life. Unfortunately, since Popovsky is an emigré writer, I only came across his work in late 1991. The book by the Ukrainian doctor Mikhail Stern, *Sex in the Soviet Union* (London: 1981) may be seen more as recounting personal observations.

Rus', whatever the term means, was never a synonym for the Russian condition, Russian people or Russian culture – as with any sacred concept. Russian culture was by no means asexual.

Back in the seventeenth century, Adam Oleary testified that Russians frequently

> talk of voluptuous disport, shameful vices, perversions and love affairs concerning themselves and others, they tell all sorts of risqué stories, and the person who uses the foulest language and tells the most disgusting jokes accompanied by vulgar gestures is the one they regard as the best and most respected in the community.[1]

Many other foreign travellers wrote in similar vein.

We have a poor awareness of sexually erotic Russian culture not because it did not exist, but because the censor forbade publication of relevant sources and research. Russian scholars had to resort to foreign material. The collection *Russian Secret Proverbs and Sayings* (the word, 'secret' here is defined as 'intimate, illicit, clandestinely preserved') compiled by Vladimir Dahl around 1852 was published in the Hague as recently as 1972.[2] Alexander Afanasiev's celebrated collection *Russian Secret Folk Tales* had to be sent to Geneva for publication; translations and reprints have appeared regularly in Germany and the United Kingdom. But the book is only a tiny part of his collection. Afanasiev's magnum opus, *Popular Russian Tales not for publication, 1857–1862* is kept in the Archive Section of Pushkin House. The first, and for the time being the only, album on the history of Russian erotic art, *Eroticism in Russian Art*, came out in London in 1976.[3] The first book on sexual life in Ancient Rus, *Sex and Society in the World of the Orthodox Slavs, 900–1700* by the American researcher Eve Levin, based on Soviet archive sources, was published in the US in 1989.[4]

Attitudes to sexuality in Ancient Rus were just as contradictory as they were in Western Europe. Ancient Slav paganism did not distinguish itself either by chastity or by especial licence in regard to sexual habits. Sexuality was thought to have a cosmic source. The female 'silver birch' interlaced tenderly and passionately with the 'mighty oak'. Mother Earth became fecund from celestial rain. Alongside the female deities of fertility was also the phallic god, Rod (the Clan). There were innumerable orgiastic festivals at which men and women bathed naked together, the men symbolically fertilising the earth and the women seeking rain. The typical phallic symbol – an animal, usually the lion, denoted by his long tail or penis – is represented even in ornamental church architecture as, for example, at the Temple of the Protector on the Nerl and the Saint Dmitri Cathedral in Vladimir.

When Rus adopted Christianity in the ninth century it experienced many profound changes in culture. Russian Orthodox believers, like all Christians, regarded sexual affairs and everything associated with them as something unsavoury, pertaining to the devil. Chastity, virginity and renunciation of sex even in marriage were looked upon as something 'sacred'; however, deviations from that ascetic principle were thought to be both legitimate and permissible, but only in marriage and for the sake of reproduction, not because of fallibility.[5]

The church tried to keep control of people's conduct and thinking. At the same time, bearing in mind the realities of everyday life, Russian Orthodoxy on some issues displayed more tolerance than Catholicism did. In so far as it was most concerned with the institution of marriage, adultery was thought to be a much more serious transgression than fornication.

Actual relationships naturally differed substantially from those prescribed. There was much more violence and cruelty towards women in real life, as was the case everywhere in the Middle Ages. Russian communal bath houses shocked more than a few foreigners. Mixed bathing in the Neva river was noted even in the early twentieth century. But observers emphasised that there was nothing sexual or erotic about these activities.

The fine arts present a confused picture. Russian Orthodox icon painting is on the whole stricter and more ascetic than Western religious art. Some churches (for example, the Holy Trinity Church in Nikitniki and the Ascension Church in Tutayev) have frescoes openly portraying half-naked bodies in such subjects as *Bathsheba Bathing*, *Suzanna and the Elders* and the *Baptism of Jesus*; there is even a scene of nude women bathing. All the same, this was in sharp conflict with the strict Byzantine canon. In West European church-painting of the Renaissance period and even later Middle Ages, the entire human body is open to view, with only the sex organs veiled. In Russian icons only the face is alive, the body being entirely covered or outlined in an emaciated and ascetic way. Nothing can compare here with Raphael's Madonnas or Cranach's Adam and Eve. Secular painting appeared in Russia much later and under more stringent control. While Italian painters were portraying the naked figure in the Renaissance period, Russians only gained the right to do this in the late eighteenth century.

West European carnivals saw no distinction between performers and spectators; according to M.M. Bakhtin, everyone was an active participant, all joined in the carnival action. People did not perform a carnival and, strictly speaking, they did not even play at the carnival, they actually *lived* it.[6] In Rus, distinguished personages did not take part in the dances and games of the jesters (*skomorokhi*), treating them merely as humorous diversions. It was regarded as sinful to provoke laughter or to laugh uproariously. There were similar inhibitions about giving oneself up to playful merriment. Foreigners noted with some astonishment that dancing at a ball staged by Russian nobility was merely a spectacle and, like any art, a matter of labour: whoever danced did not make merry, but worked; merriment was the preserve of the spectators, who were too important to dance themselves.[7]

None the less, these inhibitions applied principally to 'official' behaviour. Popular customs right up to the late nineteenth century preserved substantial vestiges of pre-Christian, pagan rites, including trial marriage and orgiastic festivals. There were many sexually erotic features in Russian popular culture. Erotic folktales tell of polygamous heroes and sympathetically describe their sexual misdemeanours, like the possession of a sleeping beauty; they regard it as permissible to dishonour (that is, to rape) a girl in revenge for her refusing to marry the hero. The vocabulary of such works was such that not only Afanasiev's *Secret Tales*, but also the less well-known song collection of Kirsha Danilov could only be published abroad in their full, uncensored versions.

Russian primitive folk prints depicted very free scenes. Although a strict church censorship was introduced in 1679 and several government directives were issued during the eighteenth century, they had little effect on these prints. Sometimes the relatively decorous pictures were accompanied by less than decorous texts. One of them, dating back to the eighteenth century, tells us that three 'young wives' played a trick on a bald-headed old man, telling him he should rub 'woman's cream' into his pate. The old man took out his other 'bald pate' and said he had been rubbing it in 'woman's cream' for 40 years without it growing any hair.

The influence of French 'libertines' of the eighteenth century spread as far as Russia. Gatchina Palace, presented by Catherine the Great to her lover Grigory Orlov, contained extremely sensual frescoes and special furniture (which is today kept in the Hermitage) on which, for example, table legs are tapered in the shape of penises. Young gentlemen in Pushkin's time could enjoy not only Diderot's *Immodest Treasures* but also the bawdy verses of Ivan Barkov (1732–68).

And what bawdy and playful erotic verses we find in Pushkin himself. Today's readers of Pushkin know only part of his work. *Barkov's Shadow* is no longer in print, while only a short extract of his fairy tale in verse, *Tsar Nikita and his Forty Daughters*, appears in most Pushkin collections, ending with the words:

How might one explain,
Without making plain,
The devout stupidity
Of an over-zealous censor?[8]

Literary criticism was also very conservative. In the latter part of the eighteenth century, young people, especially young girls, were given all manner of warnings about reading the English sentimentalists as well as the French novelists. Samuel Richardson's *Pamela*, for example, was considered indecent, and in the early nineteenth century the magazine *Aurora* warned its readers of 'harmful intrusions' of sensual scenes in Rousseau's *New Eloise*. In 1823, the *Vestnik Yevropy* praised Sir Walter Scott for having no 'seductive' episodes in his work. About the same time, romanticism in art came under virulent attack for 'sensuality'.

None of this was exclusively Russian; something similar was happening about the same time in Western Europe. All the same, Russia and the West were very different. In the West the church was regarded as the major foe of erotic art. In Russia, the foe was particularly pervasive as it could call on both the authority of the church and the power of the state. More than that, eroticism had another opponent – revolutionary-democratic criticism.

Aristocrats of Pushkin's time received a good secular education from childhood; while remaining deeply moral and even religious people, they were nevertheless distanced from official hypocrisy. For the intellectuals who were not of gentle birth, who came from an ecclesiastical background or who were former seminarists, things were considerably more difficult. In breaking with certain principles, they were unable to overcome others. Transplanted into an alien social milieu, many of them suffered an acute shyness and endeavoured to repress the desires of their own flesh. Their constant inner battle turned into a fundamental – both morally and aesthetically – renunciation of sensuousness in general as something vulgar and unworthy.

Unable to exorcise his own sexuality, the writer and literary critic Vissarion Belinsky disapproved strongly of any manifestations of it in the poetry of, for example, Alexander Polezhayev. Assessing literature from the viewpoint of some imaginary 'young boy' who had to be protected from seduction in every way possible, the 'frenzied Vissarion' denounces the decadent Boccaccio, and calls Paul de Kock's work 'squalid and disgusting'. Alexander Pisarev condemned Heine for his 'sensuous view of women'. And so it goes on.

We are talking of ideology, not chance remarks. While conservative religious bigots condemned eroticism for going against the dogmas of faith, for revolutionary democrats eroticism simply did not fit the normative canon of persons who had to give all their strength to liberate the people. By contrast with that great goal, everything else paled into insignificance. Even the intimate lyrics of Afanasy Fet, Lev Polonsky or Konstantin Sluchevsky were branded as vulgar by some late-nineteenth century critics who saw no difference at all between erotic and cheap sexuality.[9] Moral maximalism was turning into the energetic foe of liberal attitudes to sex. Any artist or writer who attempted to walk up that 'slippery slope' immediately came under withering attack from right and left.

That seriously hampered the birth and development of a lofty, refined erotic art and language without which sex and, even more so, the discussion of it, inevitably appears base, dirty and squalid, and therefore becomes precisely that: the purpose and perception do not reflect reality so much as create it. There has always been much more vulgarity in Russia than eroticism.

But let us not simplify the picture.

Academic painters in the early part of the nineteenth century did not portray erotic scenes. However, without Karl Bryullov, Alexander Yegorov, Fyodor Bruni and Alexander Ivanov, the history of the portrayal of the nude human body would be incomplete. Alexander Venetsianov created wonderful images of women bathing, ballerinas and Bacchante. As artists overcame external and internal barriers, the painted and sculpted body became increasingly emotional and expressive.

The early twentieth century was especially fruitful in this respect. The canvases of Mikhail Vrubel, Valentin Serov's *Ida Rubinstein*, the

witty erotic caricatures of Mikhail Zishi, the opulent beauties of
Zinaida Serebryakova and Natalia Goncharova, the love scenes of
Konstantin Somov and the bold drawings on folklore themes of Lev
Bakst, the naked boys portrayed by Kuzma Petrov-Vodkin . . . The
list is almost endless. Russian painting convincingly demonstrates
Alexander Golovin's maxim that no single costume can compare with
the beauty of the human body.

The same tendencies were evident in theatrical art. Diaghilev's
ballets were a real festival of the human body. Never had the male
body been demonstrated so fully and selflessly as in the work of
dancers Mikhail Fokin and Vaclav Nijinsky.

Literature was developing in a similar way. Many poems by Alexei
Apukhtin, Konstantin Balmont, Valery Bryusov, Nikolai Minsky and
Mirra Lokhvitskaya were frankly sensual. Erotic prose also began to
appear – Mikhail Artsybashev's *Sanin*, Fyodor Sologub's *Ghostly
Charms* and *The Little Demon*. For the first time Russian literature
found same-sex love in the works of Mikhail Kuzmin and Lidia
Zinovieva-Annibal. In his short story *The Evening*, Nikolai Oliger
describes the sexual experiences of a 9 year-old boy (the critics wrote
that they could not be true since they could never be).

All this caused heated debate. Dmitri Merezhkovsky and Mikhail
Trigorin argued in defence of erotic themes. At the same time, Leo
Tolstoy, who had himself been accused of immorality over his *Anna
Karenina* and *Kreuzer Sonata*, refused to accept Alexander Kuprin's
The Pit, which was set in a brothel. After reading the first pages of the
novel, Tolstoy told the pianist A.B. Goldenweizer, 'I know that he
appears to be exposing sordid life. Yet in describing it he gains
enjoyment from it. And that from a man with an artistic flair cannot
be concealed'.[10] Kornei Chukovsky was likewise derogatory about
The Pit.

Major philosophers became embroiled in disputes over the nature
of love and eroticism. Vladimir Solovyov's article 'The Meaning of
Love' (1892) had resounding social echoes. While he connected eros-
love mainly with the individual, maintaining that it was unrelated to
the procreation instinct, the writer Vasily Rozanov waxed lyrical
about and defended carnal love: 'We are born to love. And as long as
we do not fulfil our love we shall languish in this world. And as long
as we have not fulfilled our love, we shall be punished in this
world'.[11]Virtually every critic denounced Rozanov, calling him an
erotomaniac, an apostle of vulgarity. Yet Nikolai Berdyaev, of all
people, sprang to his defence in the following terms:

Rozanov is laughed at or morally condemned, yet the service this
man has given is huge and will be appreciated only later. He is the
first to break the hypocritical silence with unprecedented boldness;
he has loudly and with inimitable talent said what everyone has
felt, yet kept hidden inside, he has exposed the universal torment
. . . Rozanov has with the frankness and sincerity of a genius
proclaimed for everyone to hear that sex is the most important
issue in life, a fundamentally vital question, no less crucial than
social, legal, educational and other generally recognised, sanc-
tioned issues, that this question goes much more deeply than family
types and is fundamentally related to religion, that all religions
took shape and developed through sex since sex after all is a matter
of life and death.[12]

It goes without saying that the artistic level and philosophical
outlook of the above-mentioned authors are extremely diverse. But
to deny the presence in Russian culture of an erotic tradition or to
reduce it all to vulgarity is pure ignorance.

Stalinism and Sexual Taboos

As Friedrich Engels wrote,

The issue of 'free love' comes to the forefront in every major
revolutionary movement. For some people it represents revolutionary progress, liberation from old traditional bonds that are no
longer necessary, for others it is an easily acceptable tenet that
conveniently hides all manner of free and easy relationships
between men and women.[13]

Such was the case in pre-revolutionary Russia. The traditional
religious-moral premises that underlay relations between the sexes
had been undermined, but new ones had not yet taken shape.

During the 1920s furious debates took place over 'free love', over
whether the proletariat really needed a sexual morality. Eminent
scholars and Party figures – like Alexandra Kollontai – took part in
the discussions. Pre-marital and extra-marital relations were widespread among students and young workers. According to various
research data, pre-marital relations in those years involved 85–95 per

cent of men and 48–62 per cent of women.[14] Men normally started their sex lives between the ages of 16 and 18, while about a quarter had had sexual experience before they were 16. Women's sex lives began later. The principal motivating factor for having sex was cited by women as 'love' (49 per cent), 'passion' (30 per cent) and 'curiosity' (20 per cent); men stated 'sex need' (54 per cent), 'passion' (28 per cent) and 'curiosity' (19 per cent). The percentage of extra-marital pregnancies and single mothers was very high.

Such a state of affairs was bound to concern society. Lenin himself sharply condemned a simplified approach to sexual gratification as a purely physiological requirement, whose satisfaction appeared to be just as simple as drinking a glass of water. In a conversation with Clara Zetkin, he stressed the social and moral aspects of the problem, the association between sexuality and childbirth.

In the 1920s numerous questionnaire surveys were conducted, based on quite respectable criteria for the time. People discussed widely the ideas of Freud, whose major works had been published in Russian. The problems of child psychosexual development received fairly detailed coverage in works by leading Soviet psychologists, such as Lev Vygotsky and Pyotr Blonsky. Ethnographers, linguists and folklorists like Vladimir Bogoraz-Tan, Lev Shternberg, Mikhail Bakhtin, Vladimir Propp and Olga Freidenberg all made valuable contributions to the study of sexual and related symbolism. The Soviet Union was officially represented in the World Sexual Reform League, whose 1931 congress was even scheduled for Moscow, although it did not actually take place.

During the 1930s the situation began rapidly to deteriorate. Sex surveys disappeared, together with sociology and social psychology. Psychoanalysis was subjected to rabid ideological criticism, and the works of Sigmund Freud were banned. Command-administrative control of sexual affairs took over from social-moral regulation. In 1934 the authorities restored criminal punishment for male homosexuality; abortions were banned in 1936 (the ban remained in force till 1955). All sex education vanished from schools, and the official authority on education, Anton Makarenko, regarded it as worthless even within the family, recommending parents 'tactically to avoid' any such questions put by children and to focus attention in conversations with teenagers on love and morality without any 'excessively frank' delving into narrow physiological questions. True, Makarenko thought it useful for the school doctor to conduct such discussions, though he would have had the doctor confine content to matters of hygiene. In practice, no one even did that. A strict puritanical morality was proclaimed for society; divorce and infidelity, especially after the Second World War, were subjects for enthusiastic discussion at Party and Komsomol meetings.

This turnaround was not simply a reaction to the social-moral costs of post-1917 disorganisation and marital-family relationships. By the early 1930s society had already overcome the anarchy of the early post-revolutionary years and had restored more traditional links between sexual behaviour and marital-family relations, placing the former in the context of the stable family and the values of romantic love. But the Stalinist totalitarian system did not stop at that. In order to ensure total control over the individual it had fully to 'deindividualise' the individual, to emasculate the individual's autonomy. To those ends the totalitarian state began consistently to root out and disparage all that was erotic in human beings.

George Orwell vividly explains this process in his novel *1984*[15] (see Introduction, p. 2, above). In all probability it was not a conscious strategy in the beginning but rather a continuation of revolutionary asceticism; people who had renounced everything thought they had the right to force everyone else to do the same. Yet as time went on, the anti-human, exploitative essence of this style of thinking became stronger. If a person was first and foremost a productive force working for the universal future of humankind, he or she should produce material commodities during worktime, and at home, in the night, produce children. Everything else had to be eradicated. This philosophy was well enshrined both in the stereotype of peasant thinking, nourished on a diet of anti-sexual morality, and in the ideas of the left radical intelligentsia on the possibility of, and the need for, remaking human nature.

Art was the first victim of this repressive policy. In spite of the tribulations of everyday life, Soviet artists of the 1920s continued the traditions of the 'silver age', taking pleasure in the naked human form and the portrayal of love scenes. It is difficult to think of any distinguished artist of this time who did not treat the subject in some way or other. Yet sensuousness, like spirituality, was becoming more and more suspect. These quotations are taken at random from the diaries of the celebrated Soviet satirist Ilya Ilf:[16]

Kicked out for sexual excess.

Dialogue in a Soviet picture. Love is the most awful vice.

Do you fly? I do. Far? Far. To Tashkent? Yes. That means he has loved her for a long time, that she loves him, that they even got married, perhaps even had children. Sheer allegory.

In their satirical short story 'A Faint Resemblance to Savanarola' (1932), Ilf and his partner Yevgeny Petrov tell how an editor locks his door and bawls out an artist for producing a poster showing a waitress with breasts. 'Don't forget that women and children will see the poster. Even grown men.' The artist tries to defend himself:

You surely are joking: my waitress is fully clothed. Another thing: her breasts are quite small. If you talk in terms of foot size it works out at no more than size 33.'
'So we need a boy's size, about 28. Anyway, let's cut the cackle. You know what I mean. Breasts are out.'[17]

Alas, this was no exaggeration. Together with totalitarian decay, hypocrisy grew stronger with every passing year. I well recall a Leningrad publishing house refusing to publish a photograph of Venus de Milo in a brochure on aesthetics back in the 1950s, calling it 'pornographic'. So what chance did Soviet artists have?

Things became somewhat easier under Khrushchov's thaw, but not for long. Naturally, artists did not stop working. Several erotic canvases and sculptures were made in the 1970s (by Mikhail Shemyakin, Yevgeny Zelenin, Vladimir Makarenko, Boris Messerer, Ernst Neizvestny, Vadim Sidur and many others), but these works were either not normally exhibited or were subjected to ideological abuse. Exactly the same occurred in other genres of art. It was only after enormous wrangling, for example, that the Kirov Theatre put on the wonderful choreographic miniatures by Leonid Yakobson on the theme of Rodin's *The Kiss*, *Eternal Idol* and *Eternal Spring*. Many people were also shocked by Yuri Grigorievich's choreography of the ballet *Spartacus*.

Strict censorship existed in regard to Western films, from which wholesale cuts were made before they could be viewed by the public. As in everything else, however, the top echelons of power had certain privileges in this regard. In the words of the Alexander Galich song: 'Films about Miss B. are shown by night, every night for the powerful, for the bigwigs.' And, all the while, an underground porno-business plied its trade.

Such strictures brought the country no cultural or moral benefits.

Having slammed the door on erotic art, the Party bureaucracy threw wide open the way to vulgarity and abuse. Rus had had its fill of these before, but now they permeated all strata of society. It must be said that Soviet 'barracks eroticism', as the writer Yuri Polyakov has called it,[18] is much cruder and more primitive than the most sordid foreign pornography.

The situation in science was much worse than it was in art. In the early 1930s practically all sexological research was halted and banned; it had to start again from scratch during the 1960s. As in the West, the pioneers were medical people – they include N.V. Ivanov, V.I. Zdravomyslov, I.M. Porudominsky, P.B. Posvyansky, G.V. Vasilchenko, Z.V. Rozhanovskaya, A.M. Svyadoshch.[19] Apart from ideological difficulties, problems arose from interdisciplinary wrangles among urologists, gynaecologists, endocrinologists and psychiatrists who did not understand, and even now do not particularly wish to understand, each other.

Sexology Comes into Being

Professor Georgy Vasilchenko played an important part in establishing Soviet sexology; it was under his leadership that the sexopathology unit of the Moscow Psychiatry Research Centre gained the status of a countrywide scientific methodological centre on sexopathological issues back in 1973. In the same year the first Marriage and Family advice bureau was set up in Leningrad on the initiative of Abram Svyadoshch, a professor of psychiatry. However, when he told the first council meeting he was intending to tell young married couples about fundamental sexual positions he ran into opposition: how could one talk of such things in front of innocent young women? The Professor replied that even if a newly wedded young woman really was innocent and had never heard about such things, she was bound to have to take up some position on the bridal couch. So why not teach her beforehand? 'Hold on,' came the objection, 'if we do that we could be accused of peddling pornography.' That was said not by some Party functionary but by an eminent professor of psychotherapy.

At much the same time the Leningrad psychiatrists Dmitri Isayev and Victor Kagan commenced a systematic study of child and juvenile sexuality; their guide for doctors, entitled *The Psychohygiene of Sex and Children*, was published in 1986. Moreover, the

Moscow endocrinologist Aron Belkin has been studying the problems of gender transposition for more than 20 years.

Sexopathology, however, cannot successfully progress without a study of traditional sexuality, and here the restrictions were even harsher. My own postgraduate student, Sergei Golod, on his own initiative (although I warned him that in Soviet terms the theme was 'undissertationable' and even dangerous) conducted a number of sociological surveys on sexual behaviour and adolescent attitudes as early as the 1960s.[20] When he presented his dissertation in 1969, first the Leningrad Party Regional Committee and then the Komsomol Central Committee accused him of 'ideological diversion against Soviet youth' and he was prevented from defending his work. Golod had to write a completely new dissertation on working women for whom, as we all know, sex does not exist. Generally speaking, the Soviet people's sexual behaviour is the best kept state secret of all time. The top army command at least knows the whereabouts and staffing of our military bases, but no one has an inkling of our sex lives. Even to the present day there is no worthwhile psychological research into questions concerning sexuality.

My own book, *Introduction to Sexology*, was not published for ten years even though it had been officially passed for publication by two institutes of the USSR Academy of Sciences, backed by many authoritative scholars and published abroad.[21] As the poet Alexander Galich put it, 'woe betide the theme that is in some way dubious, non-Marxist, Oh dear me, non-Marxist.' The word 'sexology' first appeared in the popular press in November 1984 in an interview with me in the Moscow daily *Moskovsky komsomolets*; this was a daring step by the editors. Hitherto sexology had been associated with pornography in many people's minds. Even to this day I am often referred to as a 'sexopathologist'; this identification of sexuality with pathology is very common.

The Price of Ignorance

No matter how hypocritical official Soviet propaganda has been, however much it has pontificated that sex is only permissible in matrimony, and even then as seldom as possible, the actual sexual behaviour, attitudes and values of Soviet people have always been just as contradictory, varying and changeable as those of the rest of humanity. The only way we have differed is in our higher level of hypocrisy and ignorance. Thinking one thing, saying another and doing something else has become common for us in all areas of life, so one can imagine the situation with the intimate, shameful and forbidden subject of sex.

The longterm trends in 'Soviet sex' are basically the same as in Western countries:

- an earlier sexual maturation of teenagers owing to acceleration of physical development;
- an earlier awakening of sexual interests and commencement of sex life;
- increasingly common pre-marital relations and cohabitation, and an increasingly tolerant attitude to them by society;
- a steady weakening, though not disappearance, of 'double standards', a coming together of forms of sexual behaviour and attitudes among men and women;
- a growing recognition of the importance of sexual gratification for the welfare and stability of marriage;
- a mounting societal interest in erotic material and the need to include it in 'high culture';
- a vast and steadily growing generation gap on these issues – many things that parents think wanton, abnormal and unacceptable seem perfectly natural for their children and grandchildren, by no means beyond the pale, let alone discussion.

Glasnost did not give rise to these trends, but it did significantly accelerate them and, what is particularly vital, brought them out into the open, made them more visible and, at the same time, problematic. Meanwhile – and this is extremely important to realise – the sexual revolution is taking place in a context of profound and universal economic, social, political, cultural and moral crisis, and among a sexually ignorant and fundamentally sexist population, in spite of the thin upper layer of fairly primitive egalitarian ideology that is inclined to ignore sexual differences. This gives a dramatic and painful form to even quite natural and healthy processes.

The long-denied and accursed issue of 'sex' has broken its bonds and become just as uncultured, wild and aggressive as all other facets of life, bringing society to a state of shock and moral panic. It was totally unexpected for moralising officialdom to discover that young people's sexual behaviour not only begins outside marriage, but does not even depend on matrimonial intentions at all. An unpublished questionnaire completed in 1978 by 3,621 students at 18 Russian colleges asked why young people had intimate relationships; the answers were as follows:

- mutual love – 36.6 per cent
- a pleasant way of spending one's time – 15.4 per cent
- desire for gratification – 14.2 per cent
- desire for emotional intimacy – 9.8 per cent
- intended marriage – 7.0 per cent
- curiosity – 5.5 per cent[22]

To the question 'Do you think it right to have pre-marital and extra-marital family [sic] relations?', only 16.7 per cent of the young men and 19.9 per cent of the young women among 1,400 first-year students at the Krivoi Rog Teacher Training College answered in the negative.[23]

These trends are perfectly normal in themselves. But American researchers have found that early commencement of sexual life for many teenagers is consistent with their participation in various forms of deviant activities and groups. This is a feature of Soviet findings as well. Large-scale research into the behaviour of schoolchildren in Estonia, Belorus and four different regions of Russia, published in 1989, found that earlier sexual activity is positively connected with smoking and drinking, and negatively linked to school success. As the report concludes, 'There is a certain "syndrome" of introduction to smoking, drinking and early sex experience among young people.'[24]

The rapid growth in sexual violence in recent years is a very worrying phenomenon. In 1988 the official figure for incidents of rape and sexual assault was 17,658, yet by 1989 it had grown to 21,873.[25] These attacks primarily involved street violence committed by young people. According to figures of the Ministry for Internal Affairs, in 1988 every fourth person convicted of rape was a minor, while 86.7 per cent of all those so convicted were under 30 years of age.[26] For the most part, they were school and technical college students. Moreover, every fourth rape is a group or gang rape. Every fifth reform-school boy is a rapist. Homosexual abuse as a means of establishing and maintaining hierarchical power relations is, in turn, flourishing in reform schools and prisons.[27]

We have begun to write and even make films about these matters, yet we still have no serious research into the psychology of violence generally or sexual violence in particular, just as we still have insufficient psychological aid for its victims, let alone the perpetrators themselves. The mass media are more concerned to whip up public fury over sexual violence; conservative writers see the major causes of the problem in excessively liberal legislation. Meanwhile, teenagers receive no systematic sex education; they cull information largely from dog-eared books or friends.

The country has no family sex education. In February 1991, the All-Union Public Opinion Centre conducted a representative survey among the Russian population, asking 'Did your parents talk to you about sex education?'. As few as 13 per cent said 'yes'; 87 per cent said 'no'. Boys are the most deprived in this respect – 15 per cent of the women answered 'yes', but only 10 per cent of the men. An interesting finding was one of age differences: whereas just 5 per cent of people over 55 responded in the affirmative, 27–28 per cent of young people under 25 answered 'yes'. Moreover, rural parents talk to their children about sex more rarely than urban parents.[28] The overall picture is depressing.

The respondents seem to wish to bring up their own children differently. To the question 'Have you spoken or do you intend to speak to your children about sex education?', 51 per cent said 'yes' and 48 per cent said 'no' (men are 6 per cent less likely to speak about this than women). But the bulk of affirmative replies came mainly from younger people, so that the range varied from 83 per cent in the 20–24 age band to 23–24 per cent in the over-55 group. Young people, however, talk in the main of what they *intend* to do rather than what they actually do. Much also depends on the level of education, place of residence and political views (the largest number of negative replies came from subscribers to the notoriously reactionary newspaper of the Russian Communist Party, *Sovetskaya Rossiya*).

Soviet schools had no real sex education. So, if their parents are not discussing the subject either, where are young people to obtain their information?

Problems are particularly acute in relation to contraceptive culture. It was much simpler and cheaper for those in charge of the Soviet health service to frighten the public, including practising doctors, with the real and illusory dangers of modernday contraception than properly to organise its production and to train the medical profession in its use. When demographers like Larissa Remennick and Mark Tolts wrote that a situation in which induced abortion as the principal means of controlling the birth rate was fraught with danger and medical complications, no one listened. When I said in 1986 and 1987, first in the newspaper *Argumenty i fakty* and then on TV, that oral contraception was better than abortion, I received a whole host of indignant letters, including some from gynaecologists.

The most widespread method of restricting the birth rate is induced abortion, which for many women even today is psychologically more acceptable than contraception, especially hormonal contraception. Our country leads the world in per capita abortions.[29] The overall material loss, in terms of productivity and healthcare, from abortions is said to run into a billion roubles. But what is the cost to the health and moral state of women? Abortions are performed without anaesthetic, in a most humiliating way. Many abortions take place outside hospitals, in unhygienic conditions.

The number of unplanned and unwanted pregnancies and births is very high. According to official state statistics, the proportion of extra-marital births in 1980 was 8.8 per cent, rising to 9.8 per cent of all newborn babies in 1987. The percentage was particularly high in towns: 10.6 per cent.[30] It is once again young, inexperienced women who suffer most. The figures we have for the provincial Urals town of Perm (with over a million inhabitants) in 1981 show that for every 1,000 pregnancies among young women who had not given birth before, there were 272 abortions, 140 births outside marriage ('single mothers') and 271 births in the first months of marriage ('shotgun marriages'). Only 317 new births out of 1,000 were conceived in marriage.[31] The share of firstborn children conceived pre-maritally among Leningrad married couples rose from 24 per cent in 1963 to 38 per cent in 1978.[32]

All this is finally being recognised. The Health Ministry is sounding the alarm. The Health and Family Association came into being in 1990 and was accepted by the International Family Planning Federation. But contraceptives, like everything else, are in chronically short supply. There is a woeful shortage of condoms, and their quality falls a long way short of world standards. The USSR has never manufactured hormonal contraceptives, and their purchase abroad is restricted by the foreign currency shortage. Matters are not helped by the low standards of gynaecologists, who are frequently slow to assimilate new methods. Finally and most importantly, there is a low level of sexual culture among the public.

This lack of sexual culture also has a deleterious effect on marital relations. The old, traditional marriage was not a sexual union;

requirements for a wife were confined to the formula: 'Give me a faithful wife and a virtuous mother.' Men could satisfy their sexual needs 'on the side', since brothels and prostitutes were available. Wives had no place in that scheme of things; a decent woman was not supposed to experience erotic needs, merely to satisfy the requirements of the more primitively organised man. Today the hierarchy of spouse-values is different.

According to Sergei Golod's surveys in 1978 and 1981, involving 250 married couples, sexual harmony regularly took third place among marriage-satisfaction factors (after spiritual and psychological compatibility for spouses married for up to ten years, and after spiritual and everyday compatibility for those living together for between ten and 15 years). However, virtually all spouses who were most satisfied with their marriages indicated sexual compatibility as a vital factor, while only 63 per cent of the unsatisfied spouses mentioned it at all.[33]

Lack of sexual satisfaction is one of the most common reasons for the break-up of marriages. A typical letter from a woman in Krasnodar runs:

> I am 31, with a college education, I dreamed of falling in love and when it happened I married a man who shared my views, habits and ideals. We have lived together for two years in all, and now I am at my wits' end; my husband tells me I do not suit him as a woman. Who can help me? I thought I was well read, yet I find myself quite ignorant. Am I really the only one?

Many problems that people ascribe to some organic 'physiological incompatibility' are no more than the consequences of inexperience and sexually erotic ignorance. The irrational taboos on certain words, which are acquired in childhood and are erroneously perceived as protecting chastity, cripple adults and youngsters alike. When we opened the first sex consultancies in the country, doctors ran into difficulties: many people were unable to talk freely even with a doctor. It is the same within the family. Once complications arise in intimate affairs, the wife runs off to her woman friend for advice, and the husband to his man friend. Yet clearly they can only resolve their problems together.

This does not affect just the quality of family life. Sexual backwardness and lack of satisfaction make people unhappy, causing neuroses, irritability, intolerance and aggressiveness. Without realising it, people vent their spleen or disillusionment on others. Repressed emotions 'break out' into fits of irrational hatred and fear of anything different, new or unusual (the so-called authoritarian personality syndrome).

On the other hand, sexual promiscuity and lack of scruple in choosing partners can only encourage not just moral dissoluteness, but the spread of venereal disease which, in recent years, has merged with the AIDS epidemic. These diseases affect children as well as adults. Every year 14,000 VD cases are registered among children, two thirds of whom are young girls. True, the number of syphilis sufferers declined from 9.6 per 1,000 people in 1985 to 5.6 in 1987, while gonorrhoea sufferers diminished from 113 to 86 per 1,000.[34] All the same, doctors are concerned at the growth in minor venereal diseases which are symptomless and discovered too late.

No moralising can replace proper medical-hygienic education, which is currently extremely backward. The authorities even tried to dismiss AIDS initially as something symptomatic of life 'over there' (that is, in the West), while *we* had only tiny 'risk groups' that could be dealt with by administrative measures. Indeed, when AIDS was just appearing on the scene the USSR was in a relatively fortunate position. As a result of our social, and especially sexual isolation from the rest of the world, HIV arrived here later than elsewhere and was less widespread. We had a few years' grace in which to prepare ourselves. Unfortunately, this time was wasted. When we received the first news about the terrible virus at the start of the 1980s, the press, aided and abetted by those who ran the Health Ministry, only sneered at '*their* lack of morals' before launching into a dirty ideological campaign, accusing the Pentagon of deliberately inventing the virus. N. Burgasov, onetime Deputy Health Minister, went on record as saying we had nothing to fear since we had criminal laws against homosexuality and drug addiction. Subsequently, when the infection did reach us, the authorities put their trust in quarantine measures and agitation for strict monogamy. They set up an anti-AIDS programme and opened diagnosis laboratories and departments to treat patients.

Sadly, such efforts fell foul of the technical backwardness of the Soviet health service, with its shortage of disposable syringes, condoms and other necessary equipment, while the anti-AIDS campaign became bogged down in sanctimonious claptrap and social-psychological ignorance – more from doctors than the public. My attempt to address the issues in the weekly magazine *Ogonyok* in June 1988 drew vituperative attacks from the 'gutter' press and not a single reaction from government departments.[35] In the meantime the number of those infected is growing; by the year 2000 there will be thousands of full-blown AIDS sufferers and millions of HIV-infected people. Moreover, 'AIDS-phobia' is mounting in tandem with this development.

What is noteworthy about the epidemiological situation in Russia is that HIV is spreading not so much by sexual means as through the extremely low level of hygiene. Partly this is related to material circumstances – the shortage of disposable syringes and other medical equipment. Even more important, however, is the lack of scruple and the negligence of medical personnel which led to children becoming the largest group of AIDS victims.

The position of sexual minorities in Russia is particularly dire.[36] Historical-cultural and ethnographic research shows that, although different cultures have symbolised homosexuality in various ways, the overall attitude to homosexuality relates to the typical level of sexual anxiety in a given culture: the greater the fear and alarm generated by sexuality as such, the more hostile people are towards homosexuality. Persecution of homosexuals rose sharply in the history of European culture as religious and other intolerance grew; the accusation of homosexuality was also often employed to discredit political rivals. Attitudes to homosexuals depend, too, on the general level of social toleration and the perception of human rights in any society. Here we have the same logic applied to other oppressed and stigmatised social minorities and groups (ethnic, cultural and so on).

These issues have been especially acute in the former USSR. Article 121 of the Criminal Code of the Russian Federation, which in the past was also used to deal with dissidents, is still in force (as of early 1992), and the public has no objective information on homosexuality. The AIDS epidemic has reinforced suspicion and fear even more. The erstwhile Soviet health service officials attached the threat of the spread of AIDS primarily to homosexuality; even today this 'risk group' is depicted by doctors and journalists alike in the blackest of tones.

In so far as the state, with the exception of the Health Ministry, appears indifferent to sexual culture, it remains for the new voluntary public organisations and special charity funds to take a major responsibility upon themselves.

The Health and Family Association (whose President is Professor

Irina Manuilova), affiliated to the International Planned Parenthood Federation, concerns itself with problems of family planning and contraceptive culture.

The Anti-AIDS Association (whose President is the well-known journalist and writer Vladimir Pozner), which publishes the popular periodical *SPID-info* (*AIDS Information*), edited by Andrei Mann, and the *Ogonyok* Anti-AIDS charity fund (whose Managing Director is Alla Alova) both deal with AIDS prevention. There is also the Association for Preventing Sexually-Transmitted Disease, headed by Professor Konstantin Borisenko.

The Soviet Children's Fund has played a valuable part in posing questions about and propagandising sexual culture; it was one of the founders and sponsors of the Health and Family Association and its weekly *Semya* (*Family*) has published a Russian translation of the popular illustrated French book for children, *L'Encyclopédie de la vie sexuelle*. This attracted frenzied attacks from the writer Valentin Rasputin, who is not exactly noted for his liberal views but who none the less was close to the USSR President Gorbachov.

The Health and Culture Association (whose General Secretary is Dr Sergei Agarkov) came into being in February 1991; among its aims is to promote and coordinate sexological research and sex education, to enhance sexual culture, to hold interdisciplinary seminars for sociocultural, pedagogical and medical programmes, to arrange a medical-psychological consultative service for both adults and teenagers and to further international cooperation in sexology and sex education.

Unfortunately, all these public organisations suffer from inadequate funds, a lack of trained personnel and their own disunity. Much depends too on the overall political climate in the country.

Moral Panic: Vox Populi or Political Reaction?

It is evident that both sexology as a science and the state of sex education among young people depend primarily on public opinion and the public level of culture – matters on which opinions have always differed everywhere.

With the weakening of censorship bans in the glasnost era, the Soviet reader and viewer had access, a few decades late, to a number of works of classical erotic literature and art, and to novels that contain elements of eroticism, like Vladimir Nabokov's *Lolita*, James

Joyce's *Ulysses* and D.H. Lawrence's *Lady Chatterley's Lover*. We have begun to hold exhibitions of erotic paintings, books and photography. The video boom has produced an influx of overseas popular eroticism, sometimes first-rate, mostly third-rate. Soviet artists have also come to life. Erotic theatre has appeared and sex scenes in the cinema are now relatively common (see Lynne Attwood's chapter in this work).[37]

All this has caught the Soviet public unawares. Initially the authorities responded by simply resorting as usual to repressive measures. The owners of videos were particular victims of such repression. In the mid-1980s aesthetically illiterate investigators and judges, relying on similarly illiterate 'expertise' from witnesses – gynaecologists and sexopathologists, schoolteachers and sports committee officials – launched a uniform terror campaign against video culture and many classical works of world cinematography, even those that were going the rounds of Soviet cinemas or had been shown at Moscow film festivals, such as Fellini's *Satiricon, Amarcord, Casanova* and *La Dolce Vita*. According to the collective wisdom of leading Soviet film critics, officially adopted by the USSR Procurator-General, nine tenths of the films which were consequently branded as pornographic or as propagating a cult of violence and cruelty had been justly defined. Upon examination by the USSR Procurator-General of the criminal cases tried in various Soviet republics and Russian regions, however, it was decided that almost 60 per cent of the defendants found guilty of those offences had been criminally accused without legal grounds.

At the same time, there was a never-ending stream of complaints about the lack of control over video salons and the so-called perversion of young people by television. The unprecedented squall of passion that blew up over eroticism is quite understandable from a sociological viewpoint. 'Moral panic' possesses quite definable social class roots. The former apparatchiks, for instance, had a nostalgia for their own personal keyhole into people's lives, which was nothing less than a special privilege. Special privileges are not so much attractive in terms of the variety and quality of the commodities available as in the fact that they give the feeling of being part of the elite: 'I can, others can't.' Suddenly what the ruling elite had seen on their closed screens was available to the masses. The end of the world was nigh!

Conservative and chauvinistic political organisations and groups have consciously employed anti-pornographic slogans to whip up mass hysteria against the glasnost they hated, accusing the media of a

Jewish-cum-Freemason conspiracy and perversion of the young. Hypocritically voicing concern for saving young souls, they were actually striving to preserve their fading power. It is hardly surprising that they portrayed young people as objects of eternal education, as dolts easily led astray by evil influences from which they had to be saved through bans, whether they liked it or not. Typically, these groups were just as scathing in their attacks on rock music, and much besides, as they were on sex.

Finally, the public has perceived erotica in a typically adolescent way. Any representation of the naked body has been regarded as sexual, any sex scene as erotic and any eroticism as pornography. A typical example of this was the stormy reaction to films like *Little Vera* and *An Extraordinary Incident on a Regional Scale*, which contained not one iota of eroticism and where sex scenes served merely to show the mundane situation and personal uncertainties of the heroes (see Chapter 3 below).

Sensible people are appealing for calm. Eroticism, even third-rate eroticism, is not the main danger threatening Soviet society. To focus attention on that aspect of life only helps to divert people from political activity into areas unthreatening to the powers-that-be.

There has been talk of the ineffective policy of global 'prohibition'. People arguing for such a strategy resemble the heroic defence in 1940 of the Maginot Line which no one was actually intending to assault – the enemy had long since passed by on the flanks into the rear. If we simply shut down all the video salons or churn out production-line films, the hankering after eroticism will only grow, and attachment to it will depend even more strongly on the black market and criminal world.

It goes without saying that social control over the production and circulation of erotic material is necessary and, probably, it would have to be stricter in Russia and the Commonwealth than it is in the West – not to preserve our long-lost chastity but simply because in a multinational country we need to take account of ethnocultural and religious differences and try to avoid provoking political crisis. So legal and administrative forms of regulation have to be determined in the localities rather than at the centre.

Moreover, reaction by the public and especially teenagers to erotic material may well differ from that in the West. People in the West have had plenty of time to get used to such items and know full well that not everything that is not banned is good and worthy of imitation. We do not have such experience and psychological immunity; the attitude of many people to the written word and information channels remains deferential and fetishised. This imposes an additional responsibility on both the state and everyone working in 'culture'. It is particularly important to prevent 'idealisation' of sexual violence.

We also need to make use of Western experience of differentiating TV, video, film and other programmes. When one knows beforehand where one is going and why, one does not impose one's tastes on other people, or prevent others from enjoying theirs. Films not recommended for teenagers may be shown in special cinemas or at special showings.

Article 228 of the old Russian Criminal Code, which made people criminally liable for making and distributing pornography, was patently inadequate and its use engendered a multitude of abuses. Law and order agencies are presently doing their best to amend the law. The Information Letter sent by the USSR Procurator-General on 17 April 1989, 'The Practice of Applying Criminal Legislation on Responsibility for Distributing Pornographic Articles and Works which Propagate the Cult of Violence and Cruelty', stressed that expertise in such cases had to be from art critics and taken with the compulsory presence of specialists of sufficient education and experience for such work. The Letter's supplementary recommendations list a whole series of specific distinctions between pornography and erotic art.

No recommendations, however, are capable of replacing an expert or a viewer of one's own aesthetic culture. To ban or not to ban is a question that is part of the positive task of shaping sexually erotic culture. Whatever their intentions, artists cannot create beautiful erotic scenes if they have had no personal experience of such moments or if their heroes can only express themselves on such themes by foul language or in the language of medical dictionaries. Obscenity invariably thrives where there is no eroticism. As the writer Yuri Polyakov once said,

> Eroticism is to physiology what art is to life. They have their own laws of reflection, and their conventions, and their secrets, and their – please excuse the expression – educative function. To put it bluntly, young people who have seen a good erotic film are unlikely to run off for intercourse in some stinking doorway . . . Forbidden fruit will still be plucked and eaten. But you can eat it joyfully, beautifully, according to all the rules that etiquette has produced

over the ages. Or you can gorge yourself, shoving it into your mouth with dirty hands and champing on it.[38]

Sexually erotic culture, like any other, cannot avoid bans and restrictions. But its formation and education, like any other culture, must take place primarily through a positive process. Many people are unable to appreciate this, and see no difference between pornography, eroticism and sex education. The Communist Party, particularly its most dogmatic representatives, in common with extreme right nationalist organisations, deliberately exploited such moods to bolster social tension and whip up hatred for 'democrats' and 'glasnost', from which society's moral degradation allegedly came. They invariably claimed to speak on behalf of the people or, at the very least, of the great silent majority, but the truth is very different.

A representative survey of public opinion was conducted in the spring of 1990, and people were asked what channels of information on sexual issues they thought most acceptable and effective. The answers were as follows:

- special school or college course – 45.6 per cent
- special popular literature – 42.5 per cent
- special films or TV programmes – 28.7 per cent
- specialist medical advice centres – 22.2 per cent
- parental discussions – 21.4 per cent
- discussion of sexual problems with peers – 5.3 per cent
- personal experience – 5.9 per cent
- other means – 0.7 per cent
- young people have no need of education on sexual issues – 3.0 per cent
- hard to say – 6.2 per cent

The overwhelming majority of people evidently preferred systematic specialist education. Yet it is precisely these channels of education that are practically non-existent.

Even more remarkable were the results of a representative survey carried out by the Public Opinion Institute in the latter part of 1991. The survey was preceded by a widespread Party leadership-inspired 'anti-pornography' campaign under the slogan of protecting culture, children and morality, initially in the media and then in the USSR Supreme Soviet. In response to the question 'What would you say about the present state of public morality?', 31 per cent agreed with the view that there had been a sharp decline in morals; this group contained a large proportion of older people, pensioners, women, managers of industrial enterprises and offices, Party members and the military (subscribers to the newspaper *Krasnaya zvezda* – *Red Star*). As many as 35 per cent agreed with the view that 'we now are confronted with things which were hitherto concealed' and 21 per cent that 'people's morals have changed, since each generation has its own moral standards', while 13 per cent found it hard to say.

Attempts by the right-wing press to ascribe the alleged 'declining morals' chiefly to eroticism and pornography were shown to be utterly baseless. A mere 11 per cent (13 per cent of women, 8.5 per cent of men) agreed with that thesis. Eroticism and pornography worry the public far less than the overall rise in violence and cruelty, people's indifference to the fate of those around them, the decline in labour discipline, the spreading of greed and apathy in regard to the country's destiny, and many other moral dilemmas. In addition, it emerged that people, especially the younger generation (up to 30 years of age) and the more educated, are fairly clear about the difference between eroticism and pornography, and do not put them on the same level – unlike the old Party press.

The public is certainly concerned about the uncontrolled spread of erotic material among children and adolescents. As many as 76 per cent of those surveyed favoured restricting access to erotic films and books according to age; only 8 per cent were against. Some 29 per cent (largely older people, pensioners, those with below-average education, Party members and the military) subscribed to the idea of an overall ban on films and printed material with an erotic content; 42 per cent opposed it. Typically, only 8 per cent of people under 25 years of age supported this proposition.

As many as 60 per cent (61 per cent of women and 58 per cent of men) were in favour of introducing sex lessons at school from the age of 11 or 12; 21 per cent were against. Here again we see a substantial educational and age difference: the proportion of affirmative replies from the under-25s was more than 80 per cent, while it was only 38 per cent from those over 60. The portrayal of the naked body on film and TV screens similarly gained disapproval from 12–15 per cent of the under-30s and 60 per cent of the over-60s.

As few as 28 per cent of those questioned agreed that the free discussion of sex problems in the mass-circulation papers and magazines had only an adverse effect on public morality; this figure again was dominated by older people, pensioners and readers of *Red Star*.

In short, ordinary Russians turn out to be by no means as conservative as were the Writers' Union members and Russian Party leaders who shouted from the rooftops on their behalf. The principal supporters of the virulent 'anti-erotic' campaign in the Party press were mainly older people, pensioners, the military and Party members (very often one and the same people). What is more, this campaign was conducted not in the interests of lofty morality but for very prosaic and quite base political purposes.

Unfortunately, the Gorbachov-appointed Commission to Draw up Measures for Preserving Public Morality, under the chairmanship of the Minister of Culture Nikolai Gubenko, came under the influence of such high-ground moralisers and ignored the opinion of the professional experts, who warned that restrictive prohibitive measures could only work within the framework of a far-reaching constructive programme on sex education and enhancement of public culture.

The recommendations of the extended session of the Health and Culture Association Secretariat, held on 19 March 1991 to discuss the draft resolution of the USSR Supreme Soviet on 'Urgent Measures to Prevent the Propagation of Pornography, the Cult of Violence and Cruelty', said in part that

> The Association is in accord with public social-psychological expertise in that the draft resolution in its present version', because of its emphasis on prohibitive measures, can only encourage unsanctioned publications and pornographic production, the involvement of young people in illegal activity, and the growth in sexual and violent crimes among psychologically disturbed people.

Despite all this, the USSR Supreme Council resolution adopted on 12 April 1991 contained merely a list of repressive and restrictive measures and not a single word about any positive programme. Official pedagogical science was moving in exactly the same direction. In April 1991 the general annual meeting of the USSR Academy of Pedagogical Sciences discussed the issue of 'Education of Young People in the New Social and Economic Conditions', and adopted a long-winded resolution expressing concern at the state of morals in society, the lack of spirituality and other lofty ideals. Not a word on the state of sexual culture.

It is far simpler and grander to fight for purity, especially moral purity, than it is to sweep the floors, as Ilf and Petrov once remarked in the 1930s. *Plus ça change* . . . Typically, a proclaimed programme tenet of the failed August 1991 coup was to combat 'the sex and violence cult'.

The Soviet Union is no more. Yet all its problems, including sexual, remain a legacy of the 'sovereign republics'. Will the governments of Russia, the Ukraine and the rest try to come to grips with them, or will they follow the old Ilf and Petrov adage, 'the lives of those who are drowning are in their own hands'?

References

1. A. Oleary, *Opisanie puteshestviya v Moskoviyu i cherez Moskoviyu v Persiyu i obratno* (St Petersburg: 1906), p. 187.
2. Claude Carey, *Les proverbes erotiques russes. Etudes de proverbes recueillis et non-publiés par Dal' et Simoni* (Paris: 1972).
3. Alex Flegon, *Eroticism in Russian Art* (London: 1976).
4. Eve Levin, *Sex and Society in the World of the Orthodox Slavs, 900–1700* (London: 1983).
5. See N.L. Pushkareva, *Zhenshchiny Drevnei Rusi* (Moscow: 1989), pp. 87–8.
6. See M.M. Bakhtin, *Rabelais and His World* (Cambridge, Mass: 1968).
7. See Y. Lotman and B. Uspensky, 'Novye aspekty izucheniya kultury Drevnei Rusi', *Voprosy literatury*, 1977, no. 3, pp. 138–50.
8. A.S. Pushkin, *Sobranie sochineniy v 10 tomakh*, vol. 3 (Moscow: 1970), p. 417.
9. A glaring example of such 'tarring everything with the same brush' is the book by G.S. Novopolin, *Pornograficheskiy element v russkoi literature* (St Petersburg: 1909).
10. See A.I. Kuprin, *Sobranie sochineniy v 6 tomakh*, vol. 5 (Moscow: 1958), pp. 749–50.
11. V. Rozanov, *Opavshie listya* (St Petersburg: 1913), p. 322.
12. N.A. Berdyaev, 'Metafizika pola i lyubvi', *Pereval*, 1907, no. 6, p. 26.
13. Friedrich Engels, *Kniga otkroveniya*, in K. Marx and F. Engels, *Sochineniya*, vol. 21 (Moscow: 1959), p. 8.
14. See Sergei Golod, 'Izuchenie polovoi morali v 20-e gody,' *Sotsiologicheskie issledovaniya*, 1986, no. 2, pp. 152–5. See also Sheila Fitzpatrick, 'Sex and Revolution: an Examination of Literary and Statistical Data on the Mores of Soviet Students in the 1920s', *Journal of Modern History*, vol. 50, no. 2, June 1978, pp. 252–78; Joachim S. Hohmann (ed.), *Sexualforschung und Politik in der Sowjetunion seit 1917* (Frankfurt/Main: 1990); Elizabeth Waters, 'The Female Form in Soviet Political Iconography, 1917–1932', in B. Evans Clements, B. Alpern Engel, D.

Worobec (eds), *Russia's Women. Accommodation, Resistance, Transformation* (Berkeley, Calif.: 1991); Wendy Goldman, 'Women, Abortion and the State, 1917–1936', in *Russia's Women*, pp. 243–66.
15. George Orwell, *1984* (London: 1967), p. 109.
16. I. Ilf and Y. Petrov, *Sobranie sochineniy v 5 tomakh*, vol. 5 (Moscow: 1961), pp. 178, 251.
17. Ibid., vol. 3, pp. 188–9. See many similar examples in Mark Popovsky, *Tretiy lishniy. On, ona i sovetsky rezhim* (London: 1985).
18. Yuri Polyakov, 'Ob eroticheskom likbeze i ne tolko o nyom', *Inostrannaya literatura*, 1989, no. 5, p. 238.
19. For medical sexology see the chapter by Lev Shcheglov in this book. See also Popovsky, *Tretiy lishniy*, for examples of sexual ignorance, and Mikhail Stern, *Sex in the Soviet Union* (New York: 1979).
20. A.G. Kharchev, S.I. Golod, 'Molodyozh i brak', in *Chelovek i obshchestvo*, vypusk VI (Leningrad: 1969), pp. 125–42; S.I. Golod, 'Sociological Problems of Sexual Morality', *Soviet Sociology*, 1969, no. 8, pp. 3–23. See also Golod's chapter in this book.
21. See Igor Kon, *Vvedenie v seksologiyu* (Moscow: 1988). See also Igor Kon, 'Nesushchestvuyushchie "plody prosveshcheniya"', *Knizhnoye obozrenie*, 1989, no. 2, pp. 7, 10, 15.
22. See Sergei Golod, *Stabilnost semi* (Leningrad: 1984), p. 21.
23. V.I. Ivanov and Y.L. Sycheva, 'Nravstvennoye i polovoye vospitanie studencheskoi molodyozhi', *Respublikanskaya nauchnaya konferentsiya 'Profilaktika sexualnoi patologii i supruzheskikh disgarmoniy'. Tezisy dokladov* (Kiev-Voroshilovgrad: 1988), pp. 171–2.
24. M.H. Titma (ed.), *Nachalo puti. Pokolenie so srednim obrazovaniem* (Moscow: 1989), p. 136.
25. *Izvestiya*, 26 February 1990.
26. *Argumenty i fakty*, 1990, no. 4, p. 3.
27. See L. Samoilov, 'Etnografiya lagerya', *Sovetskaya etnografiya*, 1990, no. 1; Samoilov, 'Puteshestvie v perevernuty mir', *Neva*, no. 4, 1989.
28. Figures are reproduced here with permission of the All-Union Public Opinion Centre.
29. See Larissa Remennick's chapter in this book.
30. 'Lichnaya zhizn v tsifrakh', *Literaturnaya gazeta*, 3 August 1988.
31. M.S. Tolts *et al.*, 'Nachalnye etapy realizatsii reproduktivnoi funktsii zhenshchin', *Zdravookhranenie Rossiyskoi Federatsii*, 1984, no. 7, pp. 13–15.
32. S.I. Golod, *Stabilnost semi* (Leningrad: Nauka, 1984), p. 6).
33. Ibid, p. 71. See also Golod's chapter in this book.
34. See *Semya*, 1989, no. 9, p. 13.
35. See A. Alova, 'Zhizn pri SPIDe. Gotovy li my?' *Ogonyok*, 1988, no. 28, pp. 12–15.

36. See Chapter 4 in this book.
37. On contemporary Russian erotic literature, see Konstantin Kustanovich, 'Sex and Literature'. Paper presented to the American Association for the Advancement of Slavic Studies, 23rd National Convention, Miami, 22–5 November 1991.
38. Yuri Polyakov, 'Ob eroticheskom likbeze', p. 239.

2

Patterns of Birth Control

LARISSA I. REMENNICK

After the October 1917 Revolution, Russia had the most progressive abortion laws in the world: terminations were performed in state hospitals free of charge, at a woman's request. This reform accompanied an upsurge in egalitarian ideas, the wide involvement of women in the labour market and public activities, and general acceptance of common-law marriage. By 1936 Stalin decided that the country required a larger workforce and army, and introduced a law legitimising abortions only under strictly defined medical conditions.

Since contraceptive facilities and information were unavailable to most women, they now had to combine compulsory work at state enterprises with frequent childbearing. They were helped in that state nursery schools were available, at least for urban dwellers. The collection of abortion statistics was also discontinued after 1936, but induced abortion (IA) itself became a widespread clandestine practice. Owing to the mounting number of complications resulting from self-induced or semi-professional terminations, and to the very modest increase in birth rates achieved, the ban on IA on social grounds was removed in 1955.

As elsewhere in Europe and in North America, the brief baby-boom of the late 1940s and early 1950s was followed by a sharp downturn in birth rates, and since the 1960s they have been below replacement level (with minor fluctuations) in the country's urban population. In 1988 total fertility rates (the mean number of children borne by a woman during her fertile years) in urban Russia and the Ukraine – the two largest republics of the old Union – were 1.896 and 1.892 respectively, while the rates in their rural populations were 3.057 and 2.436.[1]

Ever since the mid-1950s, IA has been the principal means of birth control in the former Soviet Union. The contraceptive revolution in

45

the West marked by the advent of the Pill in the mid-1960s never reached the USSR, and IA inevitably became the main instrument of the postwar fertility decline. This was due to several factors, both subjective and objective, notably:

1. The isolation of the USSR from medical and contraceptive developments in the West, and poor material conditions for the large-scale introduction of effective contraceptive practices.
2. The traditional orientation of the public health service on termination rather than pregnancy prevention; the conservatism of the medical profession and the lack of up-to-date scientific information, resulting in an overestimation of the adverse side-effects of modern contraceptive techniques.
3. The public toleration of IA (covered by a hypocritical silence at both individual and public levels) and its perception as a routine medical procedure.

This public toleration in a sense reflects the moral erosion and destruction of religious consciousness since 1917. The issue of artificial termination of newly conceived life has been deliberately shorn of any ethical and humanitarian dimensions and presented in the purely materialistic terms of a 'special type of surgery'. Public mentality, at least in the non-Muslim part of the country, perceives a 'product of conception' as simply biological matter. Thus, any kind of debate on the point at which a foetus can be considered as viable, with its rights safeguarded, would have been out of place in over-materialistic Soviet society.

At this point, let me clarify my own attitude towards IA, so as to deflect accusations of anti-abortion dogmatism. In many Western countries IA has become an ever-present political issue in debates between conservative and liberal forces. In the USSR, the IA issue had a very different meaning because of its epidemic scope and dramatic consequences. Abortion has never been a matter of choice for Soviet women (and hence a 'pro-choice' terminology would be inappropriate here), but rather a pressing necessity emanating from the lack of any alternative. IA can hardly be eradicated and a democratic society should provide easily available IA services at a woman's request. But she must also have full access to all existing methods that enable her to control her fecundability without being found to undergo abortions. Only in such a social context can the problem of woman's choice between carrying to term or interrupting her pregnancy (with its inherent moral dilemma) be fairly discussed. Soviet (and now Russian and so on) society, with its estimated annual 9–10 million IAs, performed in poor conditions and giving rise to multiple complications, has yet to achieve this state.

Until recently, IA in all its various aspects was subject to scientific scrutiny far less thoroughly than the issue merits. I have tried here to collect and present, with due critical assessment, the scattered pieces of evidence relating to IA (official vital statistics, material from local surveys, expert estimates), including its demographic and public health implications.

Induced Abortion Statistics

In the post-Stalin era, IA statistics first became available in the late 1950s and were published throughout the 1960s. Then came an information gap for almost two decades: IA data were kept 'for official use only'. The figures became available again in 1988, when the statistical yearbook *Population of the USSR, 1987* was published.[2] Figure 2.1 shows time trends of IA rates in the USSR and some typical Soviet republics.[3] We can see a rapid increase in IA rates from the mid-1950s up to the late 1960s or early 1970s, with a subsequent levelling off or slight decline. The latter was mostly caused by a structural factor – the ageing of the female reproductive population (a relative increase in the 35–49 age group), with a corresponding decline in pregnancy rates – rather than by any significant improvement in contraceptive practices. As reported by the USSR Health Ministry, between 1970 and 1988 IA numbers per 1,000 live births decreased from 170 to 118, but in the Russian Federation they were still 182.2 in the mid-1980s. It has also been estimated that in the period 1979–85 the mean number of IAs per woman of fertile age diminished only slightly, from 3.78 to 3.64 (for all territories, excluding the Ukraine, Uzbekistan and Kirgizia).[4]

As for the most recent IA figures, various sources give conflicting estimates. The problem of registration is aggravated by the traditional coexistence of two sectors of healthcare: the Health Ministry network and a much smaller network of medical institutions affiliated to particular industries. Provision of IA statistics was not compulsory for the latter. In many cases, therefore, we can only rely on incomplete Health Ministry registrations. In 1987 IA numbers in the

48   *Sex and Russian Society*

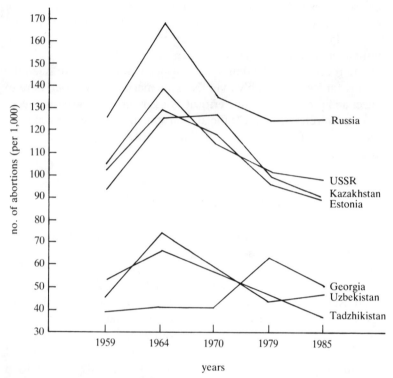

Figure 2.1: Time trends of IA rates (per 1,000 women aged 15–49) in the USSR and some republics, 1959–85

Source: *Naselenie SSSR, 1988* (Moscow: 1989)

USSR generally were 6,818,000 overall, and 6,496,000 if only the Ministry's system is taken into account.[5] In Table 2.1 IA rates refer to all registered terminations for all years except 1988, when the industrial medical service no longer provided these data. This partly explains the drop in rates between 1985 and 1988.

Official abortion statistics for 1988 were further biased because of the newly introduced out-patient menstrual regulation procedure (also known as early abortion or mini-abortion, performed by vacuum extraction within 17–20 days of amenorrhea), which did not come under regular registration. In the Health Ministry system, 1.4 million of these early terminations were reported in 1988.[6] Their real number has to be higher, since many so-called cooperative medical

Table 2.1: IA rates per 1,000 women aged 15–49 in the USSR and its republics, 1975–88

Republics	1975	1980	1985	1988*
USSR	105.7	102.3	100.3	82.3
Russian Federation	126.3	122.8	123.6	105.2
Ukraine	88.3	94.1	92.2	61.9
Belorussia	78.7	81.1	80.0	54.1
Uzbekistan	51.9	43.8	46.9	50.8
Kazakhstan	108.7	99.2	90.7	72.2
Georgia	74.0	67.7	52.4	56.6
Azerbaidzhan	43.1	39.0	30.8	22.4
Lithuania	53.0	50.9	46.3	38.0
Moldavia	89.4	90.7	96.0	88.3
Latvia	91.4	92.5	88.7	76.8
Kirgizia	84.1	76.6	73.8	67.7
Tadzhikistan	53.4	45.3	39.5	38.6
Armenia	60.5	38.8	38.4	30.2
Turkmenia	60.8	51.1	40.9	43.1
Estonia	107.1	96.7	91.4	77.3

* Registered by the Health Ministry only
Sources: *Naselenie SSSR, 1988* and *Naselenie SSSR, 1987* (Moscow: 1989 and 1988)

practices in urban areas now have the right to perform mini-abortions without official notification.

Official sources gave the following numbers of IAs in 1988: 6,068,000 overall (mini-abortions excluded) and 5,767,000 in the Health Ministry system only, with respective rates per 1,000 women aged 15–49 of 86.6 and 82.3.[7] At the same time, leading Ministry officials responsible for maternity and childcare stated that the total number of IAs was 7,265,826 (with a respective rate of 103.79), including 6,927,662 performed under the Health Ministry system.[8] No explanation appeared of this remarkable discrepancy of 1,187,826 IAs in official publications, presumably coming from the same sources. However, the higher figures seem to be more reliable. Independent estimates by the American Stanley Henshaw of the Alan Guttmacher Institute gave figures of 11 million IAs, a rate of 181, and a ratio (the percentage of known pregnancies ending in IA) of 68 in 1982.[9] Whichever is correct, IA prevalence in the former Soviet Union undoubtedly outstripped that in any other country in the world, excluding probably post-Ceausescu Romania (see Table 2.2).

Table 2.2: IA rates per 1,000 women aged 15–44 in selected countries and per 1,000 women aged 15–49 in the USSR

Country	Rate	Total IA rate
Australia (1988)	16.6	0.48
Canada (1987)	10.2	0.30
China (1987)	38.8	U
Cuba (1988)	58.0	U
Czechoslovakia (1987)	46.7	1.40
England and Wales (1987)	14.2	0.41
Finland (1987)	11.7	0.36
Netherlands (1986)	5.3	0.16
Sweden (1987)	19.8	0.60
United States (1985)	28.0	0.80
Yugoslavia (1984)	70.5	U
USSR (1988)	86.6	U

U: unknown
Source: S.K. Henshaw, 'Induced Abortion: A World Review, 1990', *Family Planning Perspectives*, 1990, no. 22, pp. 76–89

Epidemiology and Social Determinants of IA

The real number of IAs is significantly higher than that given in official sources. In spite of legal and available IA services, there have been many out-of-hospital terminations motivated by fear of publicity (until recently the procedure required two or three nights' hospitalisation with its cause clearly stated in a sick-leave document), or by advanced gestational age, or both. In distant rural areas gynaecological clinics are often difficult to reach, their waiting lists are long and fear of rumour is very powerful. It is reckoned that up to three quarters of out-of-hospital terminations are self-induced.[10]

Official estimates of non-medical IAs based on hospital admissions with complications (making up 'the tip of the iceberg') are about 13 per cent of the total rate in the old USSR and 10.5 per cent in Russia (1985).[11] Substantial numbers of IAs have also been performed privately (in the same hospital, but for a fee, without official notification and as an out-patient); many women have sought this semi-legal opportunity in order to obtain better treatment and general anaesthesia. A. Popov estimates that as much as 50–70 per cent ought to be added to the registered IA figure so as to account for this unreported supplement, which would put the annual IA total in the old USSR as high as 10–11 million.[12] I consider this an exaggeration. An additional 30–40 per cent would be a more realistic estimate, which still puts the IA total at 9–9.5 million a year.

The proportion of out-of-hospital IAs varies greatly across the country, reflecting uneven local conditions and social toleration of IA. Within Russia this variation is reckoned to be in the range of factor three or four.[13] In the non-Muslim republics of the Caucasus (Georgia and Armenia) the true number of IAs is estimated to be between two and three times higher than that registered, owing to both non-medical and non-registered medical IAs. As Georgian authors report, in 1982 there were 17,200 registered live births in the capital city Tbilisi compared to 2,600 IAs, whereas the real abortion-to-livebirths ratio was assessed at 3.5: 1.0.[14] The total number of deliveries per Georgian woman was 2.3–2.5, while the respective number of IAs was 6.5–6.8. Severe underreporting of IAs is also typical of the urban populace in Central Asia[15] and many parts of Russia.[16]

The age distribution of women having IAs is not available from Soviet statistics; neither are the distribution by gestational age, marital status, number of children and prior IAs, and medical procedures used. However, expert estimates and a few local surveys indicate that the highest IA rate coincides with the peak reproductive activity age of 20–29.[17] Although in most Western countries 50–55 per cent of IAs are also performed in this age span,[18] in the former USSR this proportion must be somewhat higher (60–65 per cent) owing to the relatively low weight of the teenage group. By contrast with the US and other Western countries, most IAs in Russia occur in married women rather than young singles. A survey of patients at several abortion departments in Moscow clinics showed that 87.3 per cent of women were married at the moment of interview.[19]

Although the total abortion rate cannot be exactly determined, some local surveys, performed mostly in Russia, allow us to estimate the mean number of terminations per woman. An overall analysis of these figures suggests that, by the end of her reproductive life, an average sexually active woman has between two and three IAs (and up to 4.5 if calculated only for women who have had abortions).[20] For instance, a study of a representative sample of urban and rural residents in various parts of the Russian Federation showed that 46 per cent of respondents had had more than three IAs by the end of their childbearing years, and 20 per cent had had more than five

IAs.[21] The proportion of women who had been pregnant and never had a termination varied in different samples between 15 and 25 per cent.[22]

These figures are much the same for 75–80 per cent of the total population of the country with a post-transitional reproductive pattern, including the European part, Siberia and the Soviet Far East. By contrast, in most Muslim regions of the old USSR (the republics of Central Asia, Azerbaidzhan and some other parts of the Caucasus), which traditionally lack fertility control, the main bulk of pregnancies still results in live births. Thus a survey in Uzbekistan showed that Uzbek women born in 1930–4 and aged 40–5 at interview had 95.3 per cent of their pregnancies completed to term and only 3.4 per cent interrupted. Russian women born in the same years completed 59 per cent of their pregnancies (which were fewer because of contraception). Subsequent generations of Uzbek women, however, experienced some increase in the proportion of terminations (10.2 per cent for those born in 1945–9). In the Muslim areas, pregnancy outcomes are strongly related to the social and educational status of women: farm-workers born in 1945–9 reported that 91.8 per cent of their pregnancies ended in a live birth and 2.3 per cent in IA, while respective figures for women in service industries (specialists, teachers, office-workers) were 68.2 per cent and 27.5 per cent.[23]

As in many other countries, termination of the first pregnancy is quite common. Official statistics on first IAs suffer from severe underreporting. We can infer from Health Ministry files that the proportion of terminations of the first pregnancy among all IAs in the mid-1980s was 3.3 per cent and 3.5 per cent in the USSR and Russia respectively.[24] Since young primigravid women are subject to the higher risk of an out-of-hospital termination (according to a Ministry report, comprising 20 per cent of IAs in this group),[25] terminations in this category often go unreported, or are registered as an IA of pregnancies other than the first. In many regions multiple terminations among non-parous women are prevalent. Thus a survey based on two maternity hospitals in Georgia's capital, Tbilisi, showed that of the 403 non-parous respondents in the abortion department, 25 per cent had had their first IA, 53 per cent their second and 22 per cent their third or more.[26] A follow-up study of 200 newlyweds in Moscow suggests that roughly 10–12 per cent of wives interrupt their first pregnancy;[27] similar results were reported in another Moscow study by I.P. Katkova and I.S. Shurandina.[28]

The problem of teenage pregnancies is less dramatic (at least in relative terms) than in some Western countries. For example, in the United States 26.2 per cent of all IAs in 1985 were for women below the age of 20, including 11.5 per cent for those under 18. Great Britain also has a high proportion of adolescents among all women having abortions: 24.9 per cent in England and Wales and 28.1 per cent in Scotland were under 20 years of age in 1987, including 11.7 per cent under 18 in England and Wales (data for Scotland unavailable).[29]

The proportion of women under 17 having IAs that may be derived from Soviet statistics of the mid-1980s is 0.32 per cent of all registered terminations in the country overall and 0.36 per cent of those in Russia.[30] This low percentage is due to a much higher value of the denominator. For the reasons stated above, the real figures, both absolute and relative, must be much higher; but even if increased by an entire order of magnitude, the level is still lower than in the US or British statistics cited. Given the trend towards the earlier onset of sexual activity, and the virtually non-existent sex education of Soviet youth, a dramatic increase in teenage pregnancy and IA rates may be expected fairly soon. As indicated by the experience of Scandinavian and some other developed countries, the only way to resist this trend is to establish a ubiquitous system of sex education through schools and all other channels of mass communication.[31] So far only the first awkward steps have been taken in this direction.[32]

Besides objective reasons (poor material conditions in the state health service generally, and longterm neglect of maternity and family planning services in particular), some subjective factors also contribute greatly to the high IA incidence in the country. Of the latter, psychological toleration of abortion by the individual and society is probably the most important. For decades, IA has been perceived as a routine, although certainly unpleasant, medical procedure, comparable, say, to the removal of a tooth. This is combined with an ultra-cautious attitude towards contraception in general, which is viewed as something 'unnatural' (in most cases this had nothing to do with religious beliefs). Such an attitude has often been supported by the medical profession, ever ready to stress the harmful side-effects of modern contraceptives (especially the Pill), but never mentioning the great advantages of a safe sex life. Given that IA procedure is brief and easily available, and ethical objections to it weak, very few women are persistent enough to follow the difficult and expensive path of finding efficient and personally acceptable contraceptives. Despite criticism from medical specialists,[33] many local practitioners responsible for primary maternity care still tend to discourage women from using the Pill and other forms of hormonal contraception because of their belief that its inherent risks outweigh those of IA.[34]

Contraception versus Abortion

In the mid-1980s the availability of all contraceptives from retail outlets comprised roughly 20 per cent of the estimated need.[35] Until very recently therefore, many women had to rely upon IA in cases of unwanted pregnancies. In a representative survey in Georgia, involving about 1,500 women from four regions of the republic with varying birth rates, only 18.2 per cent of all respondents in rural communities reported regular use of a contraceptive method and all the rest preferred to interrupt an unplanned pregnancy.[36] Interviews conducted in maternity clinics of the northern Russian city of Archangel with 680 women who had recently had abortions showed that 87 per cent of them were aware of contraceptive methods, but only 56.8 per cent used them more or less regularly. About half of all respondents in the study thought that contraceptive intervention in sexual intercourse was harmful for the health of both man and woman. This potential danger, in their opinion, outweighed the risks of IA, of which all but a few respondents also knew.[37]

IA versus contraception as a chosen birth control strategy is strongly related to education. In a survey of some 3,000 married couples in the Urals city of Perm, the authors found that in families where both spouses had only primary education (that is, less than eight years of schooling) cumulative frequencies of pregnancy and IA were, respectively, 43 per cent and 35 per cent higher than in families where both husband and wife had college/university education, while the mean number of live births in the former was only 19 per cent higher.[38]

For most young couples, the birth of the first child is not postponed: only about 20 per cent of 1,319 young couples with two children in Moscow, surveyed by Antonov and Medkov in 1978,[39] used contraception before their first birth (varying from 11.3 per cent in working-class women to 27.8 per cent in professional females and 39.8 per cent in students). As many as 52.2 per cent of women in this study had a proto-genetic interval of less than a year. Interestingly,

Table 2.3: Percentage of spouses reporting contraceptive use at various stages of marriage in Moscow and Saratov

Contraceptive use	Moscow		Saratov	
	Wives	Husbands	Wives	Husbands
Prior to first pregnancy	30.4	34.8	19.9	23.9
Prior to first birth	30.4	36.7	17.7	20.3
Between first and second births	68.9	71.6	73.7	69.9
Currently	82.4	75.7	79.6	76.4

Source: Y.B. Babin, 'Kontratseptivnoye povedenie suprugov v gorodskikh semyakh', in A.I. Antonov (ed.), *Detnost semyi: vchera, sevodnya, zavtra* (Moscow: 1986), pp. 146–56

only 8.2 per cent of the wives answered that they preferred to have an IA every now and then rather than to take routine care of contraception. On the other hand, Popov estimates that abortion-oriented attitudes exist in as many as 25 per cent of Moscow's women.[40] The true figure probably lies somewhere in between.

By the mid-1980s contraceptive use in urban families had increased somewhat, but inefficient traditional methods still prevailed. In a study made by the Institute of Sociology in 1983–5 in Moscow and two other representative cities – Ufa and Saratov – 1,000 couples with one or two children and wives under the age of 35 were interviewed about their birth control knowledge, attitudes and practices.[41] The prevalence of contraceptive use at various stages of marriage as indicated by wives and husbands in Moscow and Saratov is shown in Table 2.3. Notably, husbands tended to overestimate contraceptive use in the initial period of marriage (putting the responsibility upon women?) and underestimated it later in life (thinking the wife no longer needs it?).

Knowledge about existing contraceptive methods varied between the three urban centres studied. Predictably, the highest percentage of those informed about contraceptive options was found in Moscow. But even in this major metropolitan centre 25 per cent of the wives and 27.1 per cent of the husbands had never heard of the Pill (in Ufa the respective figures were 30.6 per cent and 50.3 per cent). As many as 95–97 per cent of women and 85–87 per cent of men in all three cities knew about intra-uterine devices (IUD). This reflects much greater positive emphasis placed by the health authorities and medical practitioners on intra-uterine contraception; for years this has been the only officially accepted form of modern birth control.[42]

The opinions of men and women on the main properties of contraceptive methods show that up to 80 per cent of respondents of either sex had only a vague idea of their advantages and disadvantages ('don't know' replies). When pressed to give an answer, many respondents revealed a poor or severely biased understanding of the efficiency, convenience and health effects of the major contraceptive techniques (Table 2.4). As this table shows, misleading views were common even among Moscow residents, who presumably have better access to information. On the whole, both women and men were sceptical about the merits of contraception; all methods had low average scores in perceived efficiency and convenience, and negative health effects were attributed to all methods except periodic abstinence (and even this was considered harmful by 35.3 per cent of husbands and 22.9 per cent of wives in Moscow).

The perceptions about particular methods were clearly distorted. Strikingly to a Westerner, only 18.1 per cent of wives and 13 per cent of husbands in Moscow considered the Pill as an efficient contraceptive (in Saratov, respectively, 7 per cent and 3.6 per cent). Almost 62 per cent of women and 63 per cent of men in Moscow, and 71 per cent and 74 per cent in Saratov, did not grant it the merit of convenience (probably owing to the accuracy it requires). A highly negative perception of health risks of the Pill (94–95 per cent of all respondents considered it dangerous) might be expected owing to the consistently negative image of the Pill created by the media and health authorities. For years it has been associated with the moral degeneration and sexual promiscuity of the West; Pill-related risks have been exaggerated and the benefits never mentioned. Those who, in spite of this campaign, tried to use the Pill often had to cease because, until recently, only outdated high-dose brands, with their many side-effects, were available from chemists.[43] Now that sufficient amounts of the modern low-dose Pill have been imported, it is still underused because of the prejudice of both doctors and their patients.[44]

Husbands and wives in both cities considered coitus interruptus and the condom to be the most efficient contraceptive methods (although with Soviet condoms, often of poor quality, failure rates have always been high). The IUD, more popular in the USSR than in many other countries, still lacks reliability in the opinion of both wives and husbands (only 21–30 per cent in both cities considered it

Table 2.4: Percentage distribution of opinions about various contraceptive methods in Moscow (1) and Saratov (2)

| | Respondents' opinions | | | | | |
| | Efficient | | Convenient | | Harmless | |
Contraceptive methods*	1	2	1	2	1	2
Wives						
Withdrawal	41.7	39.7	18.1	12.1	10.3	7.2
Condom	36.8	34.7	28.4	23.8	48.5	45.7
IUD	29.9	26.6	39.2	35.2	20.6	25.5
Rhythm/calendar	23.0	30.7	53.9	56.8	77.1	70.1
Pill	18.1	7.0	38.2	28.9	6.4	5.1
Douche	15.7	14.3	14.2	27.4	36.3	37.7
Cervical cap	5.4	6.0	2.5	3.2	15.2	14.8
Chemical spermicides	3.4	4.1	6.9	9.5	11.8	8.5
Husbands						
Withdrawal	43.0	40.3	10.6	6.0	9.7	9.8
Condom	41.5	46.1	17.4	19.3	60.9	50.2
IUD	21.7	23.5	33.8	30.9	19.8	18.1
Rhythm/calendar	20.8	25.1	48.3	50.9	64.7	63.5
Pill	13.0	3.6	37.2	25.7	5.3	5.5
Douche	2.4	8.2	11.1	17.0	22.2	23.1
Cervical cap	11.6	2.9	6.8	3.3	24.6	13.6
Chemical spermicides	2.9	3.3	10.6	12.1	7.7	7.8

* Methods are ranked according to decline in efficiency as perceived by Moscow wives
Source: Y.B. Babin, 'Kontratseptivnoye povedenie suprugov v gorodskikh semyakh'

efficient). This may partly be explained by the fact that the only IUD type used until recently – the Lippes Loop – had higher expulsion and pregnancy rates than any other; but it is still far more efficient than either withdrawal or the condom.

Hygienic procedure with the least contraceptive effect (the douche) was considered as a reliable birth control method by 15.7 per cent of wives in Moscow and 14.3 per cent in Saratov. Very few respondents gave positive estimates of chemical spermicides. That is understandable, since the spermicide products available are un- pleasant to use and often cause allergies; the most efficient and popular in the West, foams and jellies containing Nonoxynol-9, are neither produced nor imported. Very few young people are aware of

Table 2.5: Current contraceptive use by method in Moscow and Saratov as reported by wives and husbands (percentages)

Contraceptive method*	Moscow		Saratov	
	Wives	Husbands	Wives	Husbands
All users	100	100	100	100
Rhythm/calendar	27	29	27.6	28.8
Withdrawal	24.9	26.2	20.7	22.6
Condom	24.4	26.2	20.5	24.2
IUD	9.8	9.3	8.5	8.2
Douche	8.1	4.9	17.0	10.6
Chemical spermicides	2.5	2.1	3.0	3.3
Pill	2.0	1.3	2.5	2.1
Cervical cap	1.3	1.0	0.2	0.2

* Ranked according to decline in use reported by Moscow wives
Source: Y.B. Babin, 'Kontratseptivnoye povedenie suprugov v gorodskikh semyakh'

the benefits of the combined use of condoms and spermicides – a factor contributing to the spread of AIDS in the country.

The structure of current contraceptive use in Moscow and Saratov is presented in Table 2.5. The least efficient methods (rhythm/calendar, coitus interruptus and condom) were dominant, comprising together 76.3 per cent of current contraceptive use as reported by Moscow women and 81.4 per cent by Saratov women. The Pill and IUD were used by only 11.8 per cent and 10.6 per cent of women in the respective cities. This is consistent with most recent Health Ministry estimates for the country overall: 12.2 per cent of potentially fertile women use the IUD and 1.1 per cent use the Pill,[45] compared to combined IUD and Pill use of 73 per cent in Northern Europe, 69 per cent in Canada, 62 per cent in the US and 62 per cent Hungary.[46] Most authors agree that about 80 per cent of IAs in the old USSR have directly resulted from the use of inefficient birth control methods rather than mass rejection of contraception as such.[47]

Public Health Implications

IA is the most frequent surgical procedure performed in the country. Many doctors have to perform IA throughout their working weeks as their primary professional duty: according to official records, most probably underestimated, 3,500 of clinical obstetricians and gynaecologists work fulltime on the abortion 'conveyor belt'.[48] Given the miserable state of mother- and childcare in many parts of the country, and the high rate of infant mortality, this can hardly be afforded. As most terminations are performed at a relatively advanced stage of pregnancy (9–12 weeks), and as the highly traumatic dilation and curettage (D&C) procedure is still widely used (vacuum extraction is often supplemented by curettage), complications of medical IAs are not unusual. General problems of Soviet healthcare contribute to the high level of post-abortive morbidity. They include lack of disposable instruments and gloves; shortages of drugs, including efficient anaesthetics; insufficient skills of doctors and nurses (according to a recent survey by the Health Ministry, only 25 per cent of clinicians working in obstetrics and gynaecology have a full command of methods of surgical treatment);[49] and overloading in clinical premises performing IAs.

A study of the social and medical implications of IA was a traditional subject of Russian and early Soviet social hygiene, but it was abruptly halted after Stalin's prohibition of IAs in 1936 and was only recommenced in the mid-1980s. Here I will briefly summarise only its demographic and public health consequences, leaving for special consideration the ethical, social and psychological implications of routine terminations.

The main interests of the medical profession and social hygienists have always been centred on the effects of IA on reproductive health. It has been estimated that as many as 80 per cent of secondary infertility cases in the country are directly related to a history of IA, through such intermediate conditions as pelvic inflammatory disease and sex hormone disorders. About 30 per cent of women with a history of IA suffer from subfecundity of various forms and severity, most often of repeated miscarriage.[50] Therefore a substantial increase in fertility rates might be expected in post-transitional areas of the country if IA is eliminated as a major means of birth control. As estimated by N.A. Schneiderman, post-abortive fertility impairment decreases the Russian birth rate by as much as 25–30 per cent.[51] This potential demographic surplus could be very useful, particularly for large cities like Moscow, St Petersburg and Kiev which currently can only reproduce their population by migration.

Multiple IAs also result in poor gynaecological health for young and middle-aged women, and a high prevalence of chronic inflammatory conditions that in later life can progress to breast and uterine cancers.[52]

IA-related mortality in the country is much higher than in most other countries. As many as 2,020 deaths associated with IA were reported by the Health Ministry in 1986–8, of which almost 77 per cent were in cases of IA performed or initiated out of hospital.[53] Only 27 deaths of women having abortions were registered in three years (1983–5) in the US with a comparable female population.[54] The death rates per 10,000 abortions were 10.09 in the Soviet Union and 0.6 in the US.

Conclusions

The unique character of the demographic transition in the USSR is related to the fact that the rapid fertility decline in 80 per cent of the population has been accomplished by IA. For nearly 40 years IA has been the universal means of birth control for all age groups, socioeconomic and ethnic categories of Soviet women.

In as much as most sexually active women have between two and three IAs at least by the end of their reproductive cycle, and terminations are often performed in poor medical and hygienic conditions, this is linked to a whole range of public health, demographic and social problems, some of which have been mentioned above.

Although most women and couples wish to use contraception, for years they have had to rely on traditional methods with high failure rates, partly because of the biased message on contraception given by doctors and the mass media. In the late 1980s some improvement in birth control options took place, but this mostly concerned women from large urban centres in the European part of the country. Effective dissemination of contraceptive information and help across the country is the key problem today; the newly established profession of social worker in family planning has much to contribute.

The attention paid by society to IA as a medical and sociocultural phenomenon is far from sufficient, given its scope and consequences. Much still remains to be done to eliminate IA epidemics and to make abortion a last resort, the back-up method for a rare failure in normally efficient contraception. That is the only role it merits in a civilised society.

Acknowledgements

I would like to record my gratitude to Stanley K. Henshaw, Deputy Director of Research at the Alan Guttmacher Institute, New York, and to Evert Ketting, Deputy Director of the Netherlands Institute of Social Sexological Research, Utrecht, for their valuable comments on this paper.

References

1. *Naselenie SSSR, 1988. Statistichesky spravochnik* (Moscow: 1989).
2. *Naselenie SSSR, 1987. Statistichesky spravochnik* (Moscow: 1988).
3. L.I. Remennick, 'Reproductive Patterns and Cancer Incidence in Women: a Population-based Correlation Study in the USSR', *International Journal of Epidemiology*, 1989, no. 18, pp. 498–510.
4. I. Manuilova, 'Family Planning in the USSR. The Role of the Soviet Family and the Health Association', *Planned Parenthood in Europe*, 1990, no. 19, pp. 9–13.
5. See *Naselenie SSSR, 1988*.
6. Manuilova, 'Family Planning in the USSR'.
7. *Naselenie SSSR, 1988*.
8. A.A. Baranov and N.G. Baklayenko, 'Puti perestroiki akushersko-ginekologicheskoi pomoschchi v strane', *Akusherstvo i ginekologiya*, 1990, no. 4, pp. 3–9.
9. S.K. Henshaw, 'Induced Abortion: a World Review, 1990', *Family Planning Perspectives*, 1990, no. 22, pp. 76–89.
10. A.A. Popov, 'O chastote i prichinakh vnebolnichnykh abortov. Obzor literatury', *Zdravookhranenie RSFSR*, 1982, no. 6, pp. 27–30.
11. Remennick, 'Reproductive Patterns and Cancer Incidence'.
12. A.A. Popov, 'Sky-high Abortion Rates Reflect Dire Lack of Choice', *Entre Nous* (the European Family Planning Magazine), 1990, no. 16, pp. 5–7.
13. Ibid.
14. T.A. Nizharadze, I.R. Mamaladze *et al.*, 'Sotsialno-demograficheskie aspekty vosproizvodstva naseleniya Gruzinskoi SSR', in *Mediko-sotsiologicheskie aspekty rozhdayemosti. Trudy NII generativnoi funktsii cheloveka* (Tbilisi, 1985), pp. 15–49.
15. I. Burieva, *Izuchenie plodovitosti zhenshchin v Uzbekskikh semyakh. Gorodskaya i selskaya semya* (Moscow: 1987).
16. Popov, 'O chastote i prichinakh'.
17. See Y.A. Sadvokasova, 'Rol aborta v osushchestvlenii soznatelnovo materinstva v SSSR: po materialam vyborochnovo obsledovaniya', in A.Y. Boyarsky (ed.), *Izuchenie vosproizvodstva naseleniya* (Moscow: 1968), pp.207–24; M.S. Bedny, *Demograficheskie faktory zdorovya*, Chapter 2 (Moscow: 1984); A.A. Popov, 'Regulirovanie rozhdeniy v

62   Sex and Russian Society

sovremennykh semyakh', in M.S. Bedny (ed.), *Semya, Zdorovye, Obshchestvo* (Moscow: 1986); L.I. Remennick, 'Mesto aborta v struktture metodov kontrolya rozhdayemosti v SSSR i za rubezhom', in G.P. Kiselyova (ed.), *Problemy demograficheskovo razvitiya SSSR* (Moscow: 1988), pp. 86–99.

18. Henshaw, 'Induced Abortion'.
19. N.A. Schneiderman and T.N. Kharkova, 'Reproduktivnye plany i ikh realizatsiya. (Po rezultatam pilotazhnovo issledovaniya)', in *Planirovanie semyi i natsionalnye traditsii. Doklady Pervoi Vsesoyuznoi konferentsii* (Tbilisi: 1988).
20. A.A. Popov, 'Mediko-demografichesky analiz kontrolya detorozhdeniya po materialam vyborochnovo issledovaniya', *Zdravookhranenie RSFSR*, 1985, no. 3, pp. 19–22.
21. N.A. Schneiderman, N.Y. Prokazova and M.V. Sandler, 'O formakh i metodakh profilaktiki iskusstvennykh abortov', *Zdravookhranenie RSFSR*, 1987, no. 6, pp. 14–18.
22. Popov, 'Mediko-demografichesky analiz'.
23. Burieva, *Izuchenie plodovitosti zhenshchin*.
24. Remennick, 'Mesto aborta v strukture metodov'.
25. Baranov and Baklayenko, 'Puti perestroiki akushersko-ginekologicheskoi pomoschchi v strane'.
26. Y.O. Vyazov, R.F. Kalashnikova-Papitashvili and T.A. Nizharadze, 'Nekotorye demograficheskie problemy abortov', in A. Khomasuridze (ed.), *Sotsio-demograficheskie i kliniko-eksperimentalnye aspekty reproduktologii* (Tbilisi: 1983), pp. 35–40.
27. V.F. Volgina, I.S. Chushkova, N.Y. Granat *et al.*, 'Organizatsionnye aspekty profilaktiki abortov', in I.A. Manuilova (ed.), *Sovremennye aspekty izucheniya reproduktivnoi funktsii zhenshchiny* (Moscow: 1982), pp. 16–19.
28. I.P. Katkova and I.S. Shurandina, 'Osobennosti vliyaniya detskoi smertnosti na rozhdayemost', *Zdravookhranenie RSFSR*, 1986, no. 8, pp. 25–28.
29. See Henshaw, 'Induced Abortion'.
30. Remennick, 'Mesto aborta v strukture metodov'.
31. D.A. Hollingsworth and M. Felice, 'Teenage Pregnancy: a Multiracial Sociological Problem', *American Journal of Obstetric Gynaecology*, 1986, no. 155, pp. 741–6.
32. I.S. Kon, 'Sovremennoye sostoyanie i perspektivy xexualnovo prosveshcheniya v SSSR', Doklad na Zasedanii Prezidiuma Akademii Pedagogicheskikh nauk SSSR (Moscow, 24 October 1990).
33. See Sadvokasova, 'Rol aborta v osushchestvlenii'; Bedny, *Demograficheskie faktory zdorovya*; Popov, 'Regulirovanie rozhdeniy v sovremennykh semyakh'.

34. Baranov and Baklayenko, 'Puti perestroiki akushersko-ginekologicheskoi pomoschchi v strane'.
35. Ibid.
36. T.A. Nizharadze, 'Nekotorye aspekty reproduktivnovo povedniya selskoi semyi v Gruzii', in D.I. Valentei (ed.), *Gorodskaya i selskaya semya* (Moscow: 1987).
37. A.L. Sannikov, V.A. Lipkunskaya and A.N. Solovtsov, 'Nekotorye voprosy izucheniya mneniy zhenshchin ob abortakh', *Zdravookhranenie RSFSR*, 1987, no. 3, pp. 23–4.
38. M.Y. Podluzhnaya, 'Zdorovye i chislo detei v semye', in M.S. Bedny (ed.), *Semya, Zdorovye, Obshchestvo* (Moscow: 1986), pp. 121–9.
39. A.I. Antonov and V.M. Medkov, *Vtoroi rebyonok* (Moscow: 1987).
40. Popov, 'Sky-high abortion rates'.
41. Y.B. Babin, 'Kontratseptivnoye povedenie suprugov v gorodskikh semyakh', in A.I. Antonov (ed.), *Detnost semyi: vchera, sevodnya, zavtra* (Moscow: 1986), pp. 146–56.
42. See Manuilova, 'Family Planning in the USSR'; Baranov and Baklayenko, 'Puti perestroiki akushersko-ginekologicheskoi pomoschchi v strane'; Bedny, *Demograficheskie faktory zdorovya*; Popov, 'Regulirovanie rozhdeniy'; Babin, 'Kontratseptivnoye'.
43. See *World Population Data Sheet* (Population Reference Bureau, Washington DC, 1990).
44. See Baranov and Baklayenko, 'Puti perestroiki akushersko-ginekologicheskoi pomoschchi v strane'.
45. Ibid.
46. See *World Population Data Sheet*.
47. See Bedny, *Demograficheskie faktory zdorovya*; Popov, 'Regulirovanie rozhdeniy v sovremennykh semyakh'; Schneiderman and Kharkova, 'Reproduktivnye plany'; Babin, 'Kontratseptivnoye'. '
48. Baranov and Baklayenko, 'Puti perestroiki akushersko-ginekologicheskoi pomoschchi v strane'.
49. Ibid.
50. Ibid. See also I.B. Frolov, 'Vliyanie operatsii iskusstvennovo aborta na organizm zhenshchin i yeyo reproduktivnuyu funktsiyu', *Akusherstvo i Ginekologiya* 1982, no. 4, pp. 6–8; V.I. Kulakov, I.R. Zak and N.N. Kulikova, *Iskusstvenny abort i yevo oslozhneniya* (Moscow: 1987).
51. See Schneiderman *et al.*, 'O formakh.
52. See Frolov, 'Vliyanie operatsii iskusstvennovo aborta'; Kulakov *et al.*, *Iskusstvenny abort i yevo oslozhneniya*; L.I. Remennick, 'Induced Abortion as Cancer Risk Factor: a Review of Epidemiological Evidence', Journal of Epidemiology and Community Health, 1990, vol. 44, no. 12.
53. Baranov and Baklayenko, 'Puti perestroiki akushersko-ginekologicheskoi pomoschchi v strane'.
54. See Henshaw, 'Induced Abortion'.

3

Sex and the Cinema

LYNNE ATTWOOD

An article in the first edition of the new film journal *Kino-glaz* notes with amusement that East European purchasers at a recent film market in the Soviet Union were amazed by the amount of genitals portrayed on the screen – particularly those of men.[1] This was not the part of the male anatomy that struck me most in the films I saw at the Seventeenth Moscow Festival in July 1991: it was the male bottom which appeared on screen with astonishing frequency – naked and always in vigorous motion. This, it turned out, was the favourite way of depicting the sex act, a virtually obligatory feature of Soviet films in the era of perestroika.

Little Vera, released in 1988, offered Soviet audiences their first cinematic sex scene in the country's history. It opened a floodgate. The 40 or so contemporary Soviet films I have seen in the past three years represent a vast exploration of new themes and genres, with sex the one consistent strand weaving through them. Clothes tumble off bodies at the drop of a hat, regardless of whether this has any relevance to the story. As Soviet critic T. Khlopyankina observes, 'It is as if someone calls out the command "undress!" and the hero obediently strips off in every second or third frame, even if this has nothing to do with the action on screen.'[2]

To some extent this cascade of sexual images can be understood simply as a desire on the part of film-makers to embrace what was formerly taboo. As Irina Levi puts it, the depiction of sex and nudity represents 'the rehabilitation of flesh . . ., a reaction against the asceticism of the still recent past'.[3] In addition, now that the Soviet film industry operates on the system of *khozraschot* (self-accounting), it has to ensure that its product is commercially viable. A film which includes abundant sex seems to be a sure way of attracting a Soviet audience, if only for its novelty value. This was evident at the Moscow Film Festival of 1989, when the theatres showing films in a series called 'Sex in the American Cinema' were besieged by crowds.

Yet there is more to Soviet cinematic sex that this. In some films it is certainly intended to do nothing more than shock and titillate; in others, however, it serves a more serious symbolic function. In this chapter I will look at a selection of the sexual images which have appeared on Soviet screens in recent years and try to discern some general patterns in the use of such images.

Sex and 'Youth Culture'

Since *Little Vera* contains the first, much celebrated Soviet sex scene, it provides the inevitable starting point for our discussion. The film was directed by Vasily Pichul, from a script written by his wife, Maria Khmelik. The setting is Zhdanov, an ugly industrial seaside town in the south of Russia, where Vera and her friends are dragging themselves through a pointless and drunken summer. Vera's father is an alcoholic lorry driver, her mother works in a factory; she herself is shortly to start training as a telephonist. This prospect does not inspire the slightest interest in her. Indeed, at present all she is interested in is her new lover, Sergei, a student at the local engineering institute. After a few nights of energetic sex, graphically presented to the audience, Vera announces to her parents that they intend to get married. Accordingly, she moves Sergei into the family apartment. Her father takes an intense dislike to her lover and stabs him in a drunken fury; later, in an equally drunken depression, Vera tries to kill herself. Thus ends the tale, the name of which in Russian serves as a double entendre: 'vera' means faith. The young people in the film have turned their backs on the old values but have nothing to replace them with; they have little faith, it seems, in anything.

Little Vera was the first in a new genre of 'youth films' which marked the early years of perestroika. In its depiction of alienated youth and pointless sex, the cinema was reflecting a social concern which had already found its way into the pages of the press. Once glasnost had freed journalistic pens from the old restraints, one of their new interests was to expose the gap between the past idealisation of socialist youth and the alarming reality. Suddenly, the image of the enthusiastic clean-cut Young Communist marching purposefully along the golden road to communism was replaced by that of the unkempt, amoral cynic, as much into sex and drugs and rock and roll as his – or her – Western counterpart. By the mid-1980s there was a variety of subcultures which had borrowed their names, musical traditions, slang and vices from the West, all of which were copiously reported in the press: *khippy* (hippies), *metalisti* (heavy metal fans), *punki* (punks), *breikery* (breakdancers), *skinheady* (skinheads).

The apparent absence of sexual restraint among young people was one of the many causes for concern. The former Soviet Union has long had a highly puritanical attitude towards sex. When Alexandra Kollontai and Clara Zetkin dared to suggest, in the 1920s, that the nature of relations between men and women in socialist society was a legitimate and important topic of discussion, Lenin complained that revolutionaries had better things to do than absorb themselves in sex problems, 'the way an Indian saint is absorbed in the contemplation of his navel'.[4] Kollontai's notion of 'Winged Eros' – an intimacy liberated from the confines of economic or patriarchal control – was parodied and vilified as the 'glass of water theory', meaning that sexual urges should be satisfied with no more thought or concern than thirst is slaked with a glass of water.[5]

With the onset of Stalinism in the late 1920s, the subject was effectively strangled completely. Thereafter, when sex was referred to at all it was taken for granted that it could only happen between adults, of opposite sexes, in multiples of two, within the tight bonds of marriage and for the purpose of procreation. Such was the official silence on the reality of sexual relations that a young Russian taking part in one of the early television linkups between the USSR and the US jokingly insisted that 'We have no sex here!' ('Sex u nas net!') – a comment which has since been repeated again and again in the Soviet press.[6] At the same time, reports on the activities of the young made it clear that the opposite was true. In the absence of alternative forms of entertainment, many young women were apparently looking for excitement in bars and restaurants, paying the prohibitive price for such evenings with sexual favours.[7] Still more alarming was a novel new game called 'daisy';[8] the girls would lie naked on the floor with their heads together and their legs radiating outwards like the petals of a daisy, while the boys went from one to the other like bumble-bees.

Little Vera, like a number of subsequent films about youth, was concerned with exploding the hypocrisies and moral pretences of the Soviet past, sexual and otherwise. In a number of ways the film turned the old Soviet values upside down. As Herbert Eagle notes, in cinematic terms it stood in direct challenge to socialist realism.[9] This was the style of film-making which dominated Soviet cinema in the Stalin era and was officially abandoned only in 1989. Using simple, straightforward narratives, socialist realism presented an idealised image of society as if it were reality. Its tales were uncomplicated, optimistic and uplifting; complex moral dilemmas were reduced to a matter of right or wrong, good or bad. Cheerful 'positive heroes' gave audiences role models on which to pattern their own lives, while the appearance of 'wreckers' and 'saboteurs' unified them against a common enemy. *Little Vera* stood in complete contrast to these goals. The film offered a virtual diary of seemingly disjointed and meaning-less events, making no attempt to explain or justify them. Its protagonists, far from being 'positive heroes', were cynical and pessimistic, estranged from both their families and society. Realism it certainly was, but of a far more literal type. Many of the thousands of letters about it sent by viewers to the Soviet press applauded Pichul for daring to show Soviet society as it really was: the claustrophobic apartment, the shabby clothes, the boredom of young people with nowhere to go. This was a far cry from the distorted, fairy-tale image of Soviet life which had been projected on the screen in the past.[10]

Little Vera also defied the traditional Soviet image of the family as the fount of all love and support. Throughout the Brezhnev years, the family was held up as 'the basic cell of Soviet society'; now it was portrayed as a spiritually oppressive institution trapped in a physi-cally oppressive space. The film's family scenes are full of tension, which sometimes spills over into physical violence. The cramped confines of the family flat are captured by the camera in minute, suffocating detail.

Finally, sex – that expression of true love between married partners – is portrayed in the film as little more than a pastime, an antidote to boredom. Love does crop up in the conversation, but in a wholly ironic sense. To Vera's casual enquiry, 'Do you love me?', Sergei's reply is an indifferent 'it goes without saying' ('razumeyetsya'). This exchange contains the same playful irony as that which takes place when the lovers are sprawled across each other on the beach; in answer to Sergei's question, 'Do you have an aim in life?', Vera responds, 'Our common aim is communism!' In *Little Vera*, then, casual sex is an expression of youth alienation from the hypocritical morality of the older generation. The old morality had been turned on its head; as an article in *Ogonyok* explained, 'the endless eulogising of our achievements . . . eternal incantations about the boundless worthiness of Soviet man. All this falsity and exaggeration, these back-slapping lies . . . have simply cultivated an atmosphere of cynicism, an almost open trampling underfoot of all moral laws.'[11]

This idea is repeated throughout 'youth genre' films, though rarely in such an accomplished way. Intergenerational conflict remains a standard feature of most of these films, but some add another, rather spicier element – the 'mafia'. This term is a post-perestroika addition to the Soviet lexicon, applied to any organised crime circle. The mafia makes an early appearance in the 1988 film *Tragedy Rock-Style*, directed by Savva Kulish. The hero, Vitya, is a teenage rock-music and motorbike fanatic whose father is a pillar of the establishment – or so it seems, until he is arrested for embezzlement. Vitya is devastated, and in this state of shock he falls prey to a supposed mystic called Cassius. In fact, Cassius turns out to be a member of the same criminal mafia as Vitya's father. His intention is to get Vitya addicted to drugs so that he becomes a virtual slave, and can then be used to help track down the money Cassius is convinced the father has hidden. So follows a series of images of psychodelic drug trips and orgiastic sex until finally, like most of these young heroes, Vitya is killed. The ultimate message is, as Vitya himself puts it, 'Children brought up on lies cannot have high moral standards.'

The sex scenes in *Tragedy Rock-Style* have a distinctly 1960s feel, with bodies gyrating in a red glow against a background of rock music. Despite an obvious intention to shock and entertain the audience with such images, the film was, again, aimed at indicating youth alienation from the older generation and society at large. The director, who met a number of young drug addicts while preparing the film, was told that sex had no more significance for them than drinking a glass of vodka (an echo of the 'glass of water' analogy). His aim was to convey this indifference on screen.[12]

There is one striking contrast between the portrayal of sex in this film and that in *Little Vera*. The heroine of *Little Vera* is actively in pursuit of her own sexual pleasure; it is she who decides when, and with whom, sex takes place. When an ex-boyfriend tries to rape her, she furiously, and successfully, beats him off. The main female character in *Tragedy Rock-Style*, however, Vitya's girlfriend Lena, is totally passive. Lena has also fallen under Cassius's influence; but while Vitya's reason for doing so is clear, Lena appears merely to be following his lead. When Cassius clambers astride her during one of the orgiastic parties, she weeps unhappily but offers no resistance. This image of woman as passive victim is, alas, a recurrent feature in recent Soviet films.

This is certainly the case with Sergei Snezhkin's *An Extraordinary Incident on a Regional Scale* (1989), a youth film of a different type, still more iconoclastic than those we have just discussed. Whereas *Little Vera* and *Tragedy Rock-Style* are about disaffected young people who have withdrawn from the system, Snezhkin is more concerned with portraying the moral bankruptcy of those who have embraced it. The film is set in the period of Brezhnev's rule and explores corruption within the Komsomol, the Communist Youth League. The hero, Nikolai Shumilin, is the First Secretary of the local Komsomol branch. He has just been promoted, and he celebrates with a party in the Komsomol sauna which turns into a drunken orgy. Meanwhile, someone breaks into the main office and steals the Komsomol banner. When a branch loses its banner it has to be disbanded, so if the banner cannot be recovered Shumilin's career will be in tatters. This flimsy plot provides the background for an analysis of the bleak reality behind the official proclamations of the Brezhnev era about youth being the shining hope of the socialist future. Its supposed vanguard emerges as devoid of any communist idealism, although it spouts the right pledges and sings the right songs at the drunken party with which the film begins.

Shumilin has both a wife and a lover, though he seems to feel no real attachment towards either. In the midst of making love to his wife he finds himself wishing she were dead, so he heads off for solace to his lover and brutally rapes her on the kitchen table. She has just been mincing meat, and blood oozes from her fingers as Shumilin thrusts into her. On a shelf above her head, Brezhnev's image appears on a television screen; her pitiful cries mingle with his voice.

Symbolic Representation of Women

Vida Johnson has described this rape as one of the best-motivated sex scenes of contemporary Soviet cinema. She suggests that the sexual violence it portrays symbolises 'the political and social impotence of men in a system which has systematically stripped them of power: they do to the women what the state has been doing to them'.[13] Certainly this is what the director wants us to think. The voice of Brezhnev, mingling with the victim's screams, indicates that what Shumilin is really 'fucking' is the Soviet system. Accordingly, it could be argued that the woman is being offered up as a symbol of the state.

There is a long tradition in Russian culture of using the figure of woman symbolically. This continues to this day. The satirical posters displayed in the post office window on Kalinin Prospect throughout the summer of 1991 used the female figure to represent Russia, the economy, culture, poverty, ecology and so on. The cinema has inherited this tradition, using women in particular to signify the motherland and morality. We have a particularly clear example of this in films about the 'Great Patriotic War' (the period of Soviet involvement in the Second World War). Until then the majority of Stalin's cinematic 'positive heroes' were male; now women suddenly came into their own. In Friedrich Ermler's 1943 film *She Defends the Motherland*, for example, the collective farm-worker Praskovya Lukyanova becomes a partisan leader to avenge the wiping out of her family. The heroine of *Zoya* (1944), directed by Lev Arnshtam, is an 18 year-old girl who is captured and tortured by the Nazis. *Prisoner No. 217* (1944), by Mikhail Romm, is about a young girl taken off to Germany and forced to work as a slave for a German family. *Marite* (1947), by Vera Stroyeva, concerns a Lithuanian girl who becomes the organiser of Lithuanian partisans in their struggle against Nazi occupation. These war heroines symbolise both the Soviet Union and its moral fortitude. The fact that they are usually young is a way of conveying the youth and innocence of the socialist order. Though they generally perish at the end of these films, they retain their spiritual strength to the final gasp; in this way they represent the courage and resilience of the Soviet people.

In *An Extraordinary Incident*, this symbolic use of women has been taken a step further. Shumilin's girlfriend is a metaphor not for the motherland but for the Soviet state and its distorted values. To portray violence against the state in this manner, however, is surely rather disturbing. Sociologists in the West have long explored the relationship between violence on the screen and violence on the streets; they do not claim a causal connection between them but they do argue that the cumulative effect of such images helps to create a climate in which violence becomes acceptable. However well motivated, the portrayal of women as the sources and recipients of male anger and frustration, and the linking of violence and sex in people's minds, are hardly likely to improve the status of women in Russian society.

It is also questionable whether such scenes are generally well motivated. Gennady Gladkov's film *The Burn* (1989) provides a particularly brutal example of violence against a woman who, in this case, is a literal representative of the system. A group of escaped prisoners capture a woman inspector. In Khlopyankina's words,

> At first they cruelly beat her around the head. One of them prepares to rape her. Another places a cigarette lighter between her legs. Finally, they wrap the body in plastic sheeting and take her to the town dump . . . But it turns out that the woman is not yet dead. She comes to her senses, and for a long time tosses futilely around in the rubbish, trying to free herself.[14]

Khlopyankina herself is not convinced of any symbolic purpose to this scene. She argues that it is there simply because it *can* be there, because the old bans have been lifted. The many Soviet citizens who inundated the press with outraged letters about the sex in *Little Vera* would have been even more horrified, she concludes, if they had known what was in store for them next.

Prostitution

As we shall see, in Pyotr Todorovsky's *International Girl*, the biggest domestic box-office hit of 1989, there is a more obviously symbolic use of sex. The film deals with another former taboo subject – prostitution. Before the advent of glasnost, the official line was that prostitution had ceased to exist in the Soviet Union. Then, from 1986, it was portrayed as one of the country's biggest growth industries and was the subject of a spate of journalistic articles as well as films. To some extent the ardent interest in prostitution can be explained in much the same way as the interest in youth alienation and sexual profligacy: it is, simply, a subject which was hitherto out of bounds. Films about prostitution, furthermore, have obvious opportunities for sex scenes. There is, however, another factor in the fascination with this subject which does not find its parallel in the curiosity about youth. Soviet society, at least in the past, provided the majority of people with few opportunities for social advancement, and little in the way of glamour. The lifestyles of foreign-currency prostitutes offer both. By selling themselves only to Western tourists and businessmen, for a fee payable in convertible currency or Western goods, they have found one of the few ways of achieving wealth in the Soviet Union; and compared with the heavy burden of the average Soviet women, their workload is light. In both the press and the cinema there is more than a hint of respect for these self-proclaimed 'independent businesswomen'.[15]

The earlier films on prostitution, such as Baranov's *How Do you Do?* and Nikishin's *High-Risk Groups* (both released in 1988), adopted a documentary format and were based primarily on interviews with prostitutes. (*High Risk-Groups*, whose title refers to those considered most at risk from AIDS, also conducted interviews with drug addicts and homosexuals.) *International Girl*, a joint Soviet–Swedish venture, was the first feature film to tackle the subject. The heroine, Tanya, is a nurse by day but at night she stalks the expensive businessmen's hotels in Leningrad. One of her clients, a Swedish computer executive, falls in love with her; she marries him and goes to live in Stockholm. This seems at first like a dream come true, but Tanya soon falls victim to the incurable Soviet disease of 'nostalgia' (acute attachment to the motherland) and eventually decides to return home. The film ends, as do many in the glasnost era, with the protagonist's death; driving to the airport with her vision obscured by both a flood of tears and a tumultuous rain storm, Tanya crashes her car.

Tanya is depicted in a wholly sympathetic light and her choice of profession is shown to be an understandable way of responding to the inadequacies of the Soviet system. Although it has its problems, it is still shown as by far the better of her two jobs; indeed, a young nursing colleague, who seems little more than a teenager, has followed in her footsteps by the end of the film. The actress who plays Tanya, Yelena Yakovleva, told a Swedish reporter that she had spent a considerable amount of time with Soviet foreign-currency prostitutes in preparing for her role, and had found them for the most part to be very well-educated, respectable women, with a great love of life. Hearing the actress heap such praise on her role models, the Swedish journalist reached the ironic conclusion that 'women who go in for the "oldest profession" . . . enjoy a higher prestige in the Soviet Union that elsewhere in the world'.[16]

The film's ultimate message, however, is not that prostitution is a fine choice of career for women throughout the world. It is that the old Soviet Union gave them no choice; everybody is forced, metaphorically, into prostitution. When Tanya's mother (who is, incidentally, unaware of her daughter's night-time job) asks if she loves her husband-to-be, Tanya replies, in a distinctly offhand manner, that she will come to love him. Her mother is horrified: 'But that's selling yourself!' she says, 'Correct,' Tanya replies. 'But how many of us do *not* sell ourselves?'

This idea is understood in the images interspersed with the film's sex scenes. Tanya abandons the profession once she is married, but is forced to return to it briefly to meet an unexpected expense. It transpires that she cannot obtain an exit visa to enable her to leave the Soviet Union without her father's written consent, even though he abandoned her and her mother some 20 years before, and he insists she pay him for doing so. As she is earning his exorbitant fee, the images of her being 'screwed' by a client alternate with images of her being 'screwed' by the system, both its agents and its victims: her money-grabbing father, the bureaucrat who is delaying her departure, the supposed friends who turn out to be using her for their own ends. This is the nature of Soviet society, is the implicit message; everybody uses everybody in order to survive. As in Snezhkin's *An Extraordinary Incident*, sex functions, at least in part, as a metaphor for the distorted values and moral collapse of Soviet society.

A similar point is made in Tofak Shakhverdiev's controversial documentary *To Die For Love* (1990). One of the first scenes has Russian teenagers discussing the concept of love and reaching the conclusion that 'There's no love – only sex.' It goes on to illustrate this casual attitude towards physical intimacy by showing that for many Russian women, even those who are happily married, prostitution is now seen as a reasonable way of earning a living in the absurd conditions of the modern Soviet Union. The film opens with scenes of cheerfully chaotic family life within a cramped communal apartment; the husband, wife and three small children seem thoroughly conventional, except for the fact that the wife works as a prostitute five evenings a week. Again, the film's message is that conventional morality has no place in the former Soviet Union. As one woman puts it, 'You can't live on 100 rubles a month. Either you become a prostitute or a thief.'

Films about prostitution have one notable feature that sets them apart from the majority of recent films from the former USSR; their protagonists are, inevitably, female. To find women as the centre of attention in films which tackle other themes is increasingly uncommon. This is partly because, in the latest batch of domestic film releases, detective and adventure films have emerged as the most popular genres. In the West, it is just possible now for women to take the lead in such films – as Erica Sheen puts it, 'to become the agents rather than the victims of cinematic narrative'.[17] One prominent example is that of the female FBI agent in *Silence of the Lambs*. In Russia and the surrounding Commonwealth, however, traditional views on appropriate gender roles (to say nothing of the paucity of female directors) make this an extremely unlikely option. Films which do have female protagonists almost always have a domestic setting; one recent example is Vyacheslav Krishtofovich's *Adam's Rib* (1990), which is about the lives and loves of three generations of women living together in one apartment. In any case, given the current crises concerning distribution and consumption in the country, women's lives are becoming increasingly oriented towards the domestic. A recent sociological study found that 90 per cent of female respondents asserted that women play little part in the process of change currently underway in the country; almost half felt that women had to spend their time in attempting to feed their families.[18] As a female film critic told me at the 1991 Moscow film festival, 'I have to decide in the morning whether to go to the film market or the food market.'

Rudolf Fruntov's *Fools Die on Fridays* (1990) is a typical film of the detective genre. Andrei is a former policeman whose life was destroyed when he found evidence of a mafia group operating within the police force. When he came close to identifying its members they arranged for him to be arrested on a trumped-up charge of police brutality, for which he spent three years in prison. Now free, he finds them on his tail again. He seeks refuge with a beautiful young woman called Yanna, who welcomes him into her apartment and her bed – but she turns out to be enmeshed in the mafia herself, exchanging sexual favours for an apartment full of imported Western goods. This does not make her an unsympathetic character, however – prostitution being, once again, a legitimate occupation for a Soviet woman – and Andrei sets out to save them both. He suffers a setback when the one friend he thought he had in the force turns out to be the mafia boss, but in the end all turns out well for the heroes.

In the meantime the audience is treated to a feast of sex scenes, some depicting various members of the mafia enjoying orgiastic weekends at their dacha, others involving Andrei and Yanna. The film's promotion literature proudly proclaims that its star actress was winner of the second prize in the Soviet Union's first beauty contest. The audience gets to judge for itself; in one unashamedly voyeuristic scene the camera moves slowly, languorously, over Yanna's body as she lies in a sauna, studying her in minute detail as if she were in a *Playboy* centrefold. As feminist film theorists have said of dominant

Hollywood cinema, the woman is offered as the object of 'the gaze', of sexual pleasure in looking.[19] The camera, exploring Yanna's body in this way, represents the eyes of the male spectator. Women in the audience have little choice but to identify with this male objectification of woman.

Sexual Violence

This excursion into soft porn is still more prominent in *Blown Kiss* (1990), directed by Abai Kaprykov. The film is so foolish it would not be worth writing about, were it not for the fact that it has received the serious attention of some Soviet critics (Yelena Stishova, for example, approvingly describes the film's star as a new Soviet Bardot),[20] and because it makes an alarming link between sex and violence. The protagonist, Nastya, is a young nurse in a rural seaside hospital. She is soon to be married to one of the hospital's surgeons, Sergei, but he refuses to consummate their relationship until their wedding night. Nastya, in the meantime, hangs on a knife-edge of sexual tension. She spends her time wandering round the hospital corridors in a lowcut uniform which displays her cleavage to best effect, taking showers with the other nurses (in one particularly scopofilic scene the screen is filled with naked breasts) and flirting with the hospital gardener and a variety of patients. When they mistakenly interpret her sexual posturing as an invitation, she gets scared and fights them off in a flurry of flesh and underwear. However, one patient – a bandage-festooned racing driver (surely some sexual symbolism here!) – is not fought off. He and Nastya enjoy a number of romps in his hospital bed until he is suddenly transferred to another hospital. This upsets Nastya so much that she contemplates suicide. She has an old hunting rifle in her apartment and, after experimenting with a number of positions, ends up pointing the barrel *between her legs*; then, at the last moment, she abandons the project. Her sexual interest in Sergei, which had been flagging, is revived when he confesses to her that he once raped a woman, which seems to reassure her that he is after all a normal hot-blooded male. The final scene is an evident metaphor for violent sexual intercourse. The couple are pictured zooming along a sea road on his motorbike; Nastya is imploring Sergei to slow down, but he ignores her. Inevitably they crash; she is thrown on to the beach and when he drags himself over to see how she is, she pulls him into a sexual embrace. She then promptly dies in his arms. Although Nastya is depicted as a woman with her own active sexuality, the unavoidable message is that women admire men who take control of them and treat them roughly.

This equation of sex and male violence is, unfortunately, finding increasing resonance not only in new films but also in new Soviet publications. The scene in which Nastya attempts suicide in *Blown Kiss* is evidently linking the rifle and the male organ; in other words, the penis is portrayed as a weapon. A similar image appeared simultaneously on street corners throughout Moscow on the back cover of the popular independent current affairs magazine *Stolitsa* (*Capital City*); a full-page photograph shows an attractive, slinkily clad woman holding a gun to her mouth,[21] an unambiguous metaphor for oral sex. In both film and magazine, the woman is portrayed as a willing participant in this threatened violence.

The notion that 'women like it rough' is repeated with particular zeal in the new spate of adventure films. One popular theme is for women to fall in love with their abusers. In Sergei Ashkenazi's film *The Hostage* (1990), for example, a young woman is taken hostage by an escaped prisoner and compelled to live with him in a mountain hut. She attempts to escape a few times, which gives him the excuse to manhandle her, but then she falls in love with him, and by the end is trying to protect him from the police who have come to rescue her.

A similar idea forms the central theme of *The Assassin* (1990), by Victor Sergeyev. In an unusual twist for a Russian adventure film, the protagonist is a woman – and a tough, independent woman at that. Olga is a news photographer who lives by herself in a spacious flat in Leningrad. She has recently attended a party at a country house outside Leningrad, where she was subjected to some kind of sexual abuse (we are given no details) by four men. She is determined to get her revenge. Rather than turn to the police – contemporary Russian films reflect a general disillusionment with the official security services – she decides to take the law into her own hands and hires a member of the local mafia to arrange a fitting punishment for her abusers. She gives no specifications as to what form this punishment should take, but stipulates only that it should be sufficient to make them remember forever what they did to her. This turns out to be a fatal mistake.

The first punishment is the gang rape of the teenage daughter of one of the men. Olga is brought to witness the good work of her employees; she is appalled, but none the less hands over the agreed fee. She phones the girl's father and tells him to assure his friends that equally grisly punishments face them. They meet, panicstricken, and despatch their youngest member, a postgraduate student called Andrei (played, incidentally, by Andrei Sokolov, *Little Vera*'s lover), to persuade her to abandon her revenge. In anger she stabs him, but then repents and gets a doctor friend to treat him. She is assured he will survive, but he cannot be moved from her flat for some time. Olga is thus forced into the position of looking after her onetime abuser, and begins to fall for him.

In the meantime, the second punishment is meted out. Victim no. 2 is kidnapped and subjected to a series of morphine injections until he is reduced to a state of hopeless addiction. Olga, now in love with Andrei, tries to call the mafia off, but inexplicably they insist on finishing the job she commissioned them to do. The third victim's car is sabotaged and he has a fatal crash. Olga, terrified now for Andrei's safety, attempts to save him by moving him from one hiding place to another. She fails, and he is stabbed to death. The film ends with Olga shooting first the mafia boss and then herself.

As a thriller, *The Assassin* works well; it is a gripping, heart-stopping tale. Of the Soviet films on sale to foreign buyers at the Seventeenth Film Festival, it was reputedly one of the most success-ful. However, it contains a number of highly dubious concepts. Firstly, there is the change in status of Olga herself; although she begins by controlling the situation, she ends up its victim. The independent woman of Hollywood's film noir always paid in the end for her independence. It could be argued that Olga, too, is punished for daring to challenge male hegemony.

Secondly, Andrei's character is rather disturbing. Recuperating in Olga's apartment, he proves himself to be a real charmer; as Olga fondly murmers, 'He's just a child.' Thus his part in the supposed sexual abuse at the start of the film becomes impossible to understand – unless such abuse is seen as nothing more than a male prank, a mere sexual misdemeanour.

Thirdly, the film contains a number of juxtaposed images which seem to contrast Olga's involvement with the dangerous underworld with more appropriate female pursuits. For example, her first meeting with the mafia boss takes place in the restaurant which he manages; while she is outlining her proposals for revenge, the camera moves to a troupe of shapely female dancers rehearsing on stage in front of them, whose femininity jars with Olga's far-from-feminine plans. Olga evidently has a feminine side to her, however; she has a huge, much-loved, fluffy toy animal, a childhood gift from her father. This provides an opportunity for flashbacks of Olga as an innocent, braided child clutching this toy, interspersed with scenes from the harsh world she now inhabits. Eisenstein used the same trick in his 1928 film *October* to indicate his disdain for women soldiers, when he juxtaposed images of women at bayonet practice with statues of a mother and child and of two lovers embracing.

Sexual and State Hypocrisy

Another thriller which places a woman in the forefront of the action, and gives her a similarly unfeminine role, is Odzhagov's *Seven Days After Murder* (1990). A young woman, Darya, is murdered at the country home of her father, who is a wealthy government official. The family's trusted, longtime chauffeur, an Azeri called Ralf, is charged with the murder; it transpires that he had been in love with the victim and was supposedly consumed with jealousy when she marries someone else. However, the audience is uncomfortably aware that there is a flaw in this easy verdict.

As the film explores the lives of its characters, a few flaws also emerge in this supposedly perfect family. The warmth and support it exudes is merely a cover; so too is its apparent moral purity. Underneath lurks a mass of vices, hatreds, jealousies and hugely inflated egos. Darya turns out to have been a drug addict, getting her supplies both from Ralf and from her elder sister Lena, a medical doctor. Both sisters have had illicit affairs with the driver, who it appears is the real father of Lena's small child. Whereas Darya was using Ralf as a casual supplier of sex as well as drugs, Lena's feelings apparently go deeper – though not deep enough for her to risk social disapprobation by marrying someone so far beneath her station. All the same, it was she who murdered Darya in a fit of jealousy when she found her in bed with Ralf. There was, unfortunately, a witness to the crime, the drunken gardener of the neighbouring dacha; but a few bottles of spirits buy his silence. Although Lena is unhappy at the thought of Ralf taking the blame for her, the final scene has her casting an interested eye over the new driver, a young Uzbek – Oriental men, it seems, are her weakness. Once more, the film exposes the hypocrisy of Soviet society and especially of its 'basic cell', the family. Sex here is an expression of the complete moral bankruptcy of this society.

Irakly Kvirikadze's *Comrade Stalin's Trip to Africa* (1990) reminds viewers that this moral turpitude is not just a byproduct of perestroika. His comic satire is set four decades earlier, in 1953. Stalin, it seems, is tired of standing on Lenin's mausoleum waving at passing processions and of travelling to all those fledgling socialist nations in the Third World. He just wants to be left in peace. He is shortly due to visit Africa, but has no intention of going; accordingly, the NKVD (the forerunner of the KGB) has to find him a double. It comes up with Moshe, a diffident Georgian Jew, and sets about training him to walk and talk like Stalin.

The sex in this film – of which there is plenty – is, once again, an expression of hypocrisy and immorality as well as abuse of power. The NKVD lieutenant in charge of Moshe's training, who is the principal representative of the Soviet system throughout the film, turns continually to his secretary for sexual relief. The position in which this action is performed, as well as its haste, suggest that she functions as little more than a sexual urinal; this offers a new variation on the 'sex as glass of water' theme. Their semi-clothed couplings are filmed against a backdrop of portraits of Marx, and on one occasion the lieutenant, a man of modest stature, even has to stand on copies of the guru's *Collected Works*. The symbolism here is obvious: respect for Marx might be mouthed by the leaders but is certainly not practised. Moshe's sexuality also comes under scrutiny, since he must take on *all* of Comrade Stalin's functions. These include his less-publicised activities with foreign female comrades. This might be a problem, since Moshe turns out to have a potency problem. However, he confesses that even before he was chosen as Stalin's stand-in he would dress up like him when he was with his girlfriend and was then sufficiently inspired to be able to perform. Again, the implication might be that Stalin 'fucked' the people in a more than literal sense.

The process of Moshe's training forms the substance of the film, allowing the director a wealth of opportunities to satirise both the leader and the society he created. Finally, just as Moshe is ready for his trip to Africa, word comes that Stalin has died. Obviously there is no point in now having a double; Moshe is given a gun and ten minutes in which to kill himself. In the meantime, the NKVD lieutenant drops in for another hasty session with his secretary. In this instance, sex is a symbol of complete moral indifference.

Women on the Other Side of the Camera

So far the films we have discussed have all had male directors. What about films made by women? Directing in the Soviet Union has always been a predominantly male profession; when Larissa Shipitko, who became one of the most celebrated Soviet directors of the 1970s, applied to the directing faculty at the Institute of Cinematography in Moscow (VGIK), she was apparently told that directing was too masculine a profession for a woman and she should try the acting department instead.[22] There have, none the less, been a number of significant female directors emerging over the years. Shipitko was killed in a car-crash in 1979; Dinara Asanova, who made a series of films about troubled youth long before perestroika, also died young. The Georgian director Lana Gogoberidze made one of the most notable films of the Brezhnev era, *Some Interviews on Personal Questions* (1979), which explores the problems women face in trying to combine a career with family life, but it is some time since she completed her last film. Kira Muratova's work was suppressed throughout the Brezhnev years – *Brief Encounters*, made in 1968, and *Long Farewells*, made in 1971, were only released in 1987 after spending almost two decades on the censor's shelf – and she is having little more luck in the era of perestroika. Her latest film, *The Asthenic Syndrome* (1990), has appeared on the screens of only a few private cinema clubs. I have not been able to see it, but gather that although its chief protagonist is a man, there is a subplot featuring a far from passive woman. In fact, one of the film's main features is, as the young Soviet critic Marina Drozdova puts it, an inversion of gender roles[23] – contrasting the passivity of the male hero with the woman's aggression. It is the woman who swears like a trooper, who seduces a stranger and then, thinking better of it, kicks him out of bed. It is worth pondering the fact that this film has not been given general release, in contrast to those depicting men dealing rape and violence to women.

The Association of Women Cinematographers did put on an afternoon of work by women directors at the 1991 Moscow Film Festival, most of which consisted of short documentaries. The one feature film was a strange offering by Natalya Kupakozova. Its title would literally be translated as 'The Wild Beach', but it appeared in the programme notes as *Picnic on the Beach*. The action takes place in the space of a single afternoon, on a beach near a provincial resort town. The characters consist of three local young men, the girlfriend of one of them, her young daughter, a streetwise visitor from Moscow, and the town simpleton; the scene is also overlooked by a soldier brandishing a rifle from a lookout tower. The young woman's body is the focus of attention during much of the film, and the Muscovite is increasingly determined to have her. He finally drags her off into the sand dunes with the help of two of the other men, while the boyfriend, angry but mute, stays behind. 'You would give me to anyone!' the woman explodes when she stumbles back to him, as if she sees herself as his possession. It is he who dies at the end of the film, though it is not clear whether he drowns accidentally or has been shot by the mysterious soldier. What the director intended to say is unfathomable (at least to this viewer) but, whatever the film's intention, the images it contains are extremely disturbing. Once again, the woman is the object of the male gaze; even though the director is female, we have no choice but to observe the action through male eyes. Once again, she is the passive victim of male violence.

Woman as Object

What conclusions can we draw from this motley assortment of sexual images in contemporary Russian cinema? It is important to reiterate first that, despite the exceptions we have noted, most of these current films have male heroes and explore male experience. Women generally appear as the central characters only in films about the family and home. In adventure films, men control the flow of the narrative; women's function is to be looked at, to provide sexual interest. Women in the audience thus have little option but to identify with the male hero. What feminist film theorist Annette Kuhn has said of her experience of Western cinema applies equally to that of the Soviet Union: she came to realise that 'my enjoyment of the movies had depended in large measure on identification with male characters. I had, that is, been putting myself in the place of the man, the hero, in order to enjoy – perhaps even to understand – films.'[24]

A number of the new adventure films do depict women as apparently independent, sometimes even living in their own apartments (a real rarity in the former Soviet Union), and seemingly in control of their own lives. However, this independence turns out to be illusory.[25] Either it is based on their sexual relationships with men (as in *Fools Die on Fridays* and *International Girl*), or it is relinquished when they fall in love with the hero (*The Assassin*). The heroine of *Little Vera*, although she has little control over other aspects of her life, does at least seem to control her own sexuality; however, she is still presented as sexual spectacle (it is she who walks around naked, not Sergei; it is her body the camera focuses on while they are making love, not his). She also pays the price for her independence, being brought to the brink of suicide by the end of the film. Olga, in *The Assassin*, tries to assert control over her sexuality by punishing those who have violated it; yet she too pays the price for daring to challenge male control. In this respect, the few active women who appear in contemporary Russian films suffer the same fate as their counterparts of Western film tradition. Either their independence is neutralised by union with the hero, or, as with the heroines of film noir, it is punished by violence. In the latter case, as Ann Kaplan puts it: 'The gun or knife stands in for the phallus which must dominate [the woman] by eliminating her.'[26]

The one exception to this rule among the films I have seen is that of Lena, in *Seven Days After Murder*. Here the woman epitomises the moral bankruptcy which, according to many Russians, is consuming the country. Since the pessimistic message is that this state of affairs is not likely to end in the near future, Lena has to be allowed to survive. This is not the only film, incidentally, to make such a statement. The clearest example is to be found in Victor Aristov's *Satan* (1990), in which the male protagonist is a latterday Raskolnikov (Dostoyevsky's anti-hero in *Crime and Punishment*), who murders the young daughter of his lover just to show he can do so. He, too, survives; the final scene has him grinning at the audience demonically, a silent threat that he will repeat his crime.

To some extent the pattern of active male/passive female, and the punishment of women who attempt to challenge this dichotomy, might be explained by the fact that the majority of films are made by men. However, I have mentioned one film directed by a woman which does nothing to defy the pattern. That female directors should endeavour to make films which fit into a masculine mould is hardly surprising in the old Soviet Union, a country which, despite long-standing proclamations about female equality, has consistently de-valued women. Indeed, the term 'female' is virtually seen as synonymous with 'inferior', which explains why women film-makers approvingly describe their more successful female colleagues as having 'a man's hand'.[27] Perhaps this also accounts for the fact that Natalya Kupakozova's *Picnic on the Beach* repeats the familiar pattern of presenting woman as the object of male gaze and the victim of male violence.

Current domestically produced films are full of images of male violence against women. There are a number of ways in which we can attempt to explain this. One is simply that the cinema, having turned its back on socialist realism, has embraced a different kind of realism with a vengeance; in place of the former idealisation of society, the negative aspects now tumble across the screen. Youth alienation, prostitution, moral anarchy, criminality and drug abuse, as well as violence, now form the basic themes of the contemporary cinema. Certainly, these problems do exist in Russian society. However, it could be argued that the pendulum has swung too far in this direction; in place of the past idealisation of Soviet society, we now find its total condemnation. As Khlopyankina puts it:

> For a long time we . . . planted in [the audience's] consciousness the myth of some kind of special Soviet character. We showed it a luscious fake lawn and said, 'this is your life'. Now we are leading it to a rubbish dump . . . and replacing one illusion with another.[28]

In some films the violence on screen, although ostensibly directed against women, is actually intended for the state, for which the woman functions as metaphor. The classic example is Snezhkin's *An Extraordinary Incident on a Regional Scale*. This is in keeping with the longstanding Russian cultural tradition of using the figure of woman in a symbolic way, especially as a symbol of the motherland and as a standard of morality. It also fits in with the other symbolic uses of sex which we have mentioned: sex as metaphor for boredom, frustration, moral breakdown and so on. In many cases, however, woman herself is evidently the intended victim of male violence – not just woman-as-symbol. At the risk of oversimplifying a complex subject, we can turn to feminist film theory for another possible explanation as to why violence against women is suddenly so popular.

A Shift in Gender Relations?

Feminist film theory is rooted in psychoanalysis. It holds that there is more to films than just the literal narrative which we see unfolding on screen. Like the human mind, films contain a hidden, 'unconscious' layer of meaning. Whereas the individual unconscious contains the traumas of childhood, the film's unconscious level rests on the myths which form the basis of, and help perpetuate, patriarchy. In Kaplan's words, 'film narratives, like dreams, symbolize a latent, repressed content, except that now the "content" refers not to an individual unconscious but to that of patriarchy in general'.[29] This is not to say that film-makers actually intend to incorporate such meanings into their work; they may merely be expressions of their own unconscious.[30]

Oedipal trends figure strongly in the cinematic subtext. Female sexuality – indeed, sexual difference – represents a threat to men as individuals, since it confronts them with the possibility of their own castration. Similarly, sexually independent women represent a threat to patriarchy by subverting the traditional order of gender relations. Thus they have to be neutralised. Before the women's movement, representing this on screen was an easier matter since women who were sexually independent were automatically 'bad' and inevitably moved in bad circles. Hence their destruction was easily explained and justified within the film narrative. This was the case with film noir heroines of the 1940s and 1950s. With the onset of the women's movement, however, women were able to claim their own sexuality and to reject this definition of themselves as bad simply because they were sexual. This meant that the reason for their punishment necessarily became more open; they were now clearly paying the price not for being bad but merely for laying claim to their own sexuality. In film noir, the gun or knife stood in for the phallus and was the means by which man reasserted control. Now the phallus was used, quite literally, as a weapon. Accordingly, as feminist film theorists have noted, there was a sudden glut of films appearing in the early 1970s which depicted women being raped.[31]

We are now finding a similar onslaught of violent images in Russia and the Commonwealth today, some two decades later. We cannot point to exactly the same cause, however. There is no Russian women's movement to speak of yet; independent women's groups have begun to emerge but they are too fragmented to constitute a movement. All the same, even without such a movement there is evident concern that patriarchy is under threat. From the mid-1970s on, alarm was expressed in the Soviet press about the 'masculinisation' of women and the challenge this posed both to Soviet manhood and to Soviet society – this legacy continues.[32] Women's over-involvement in the world outside the family (more than 90 per cent of adult Russian women go out to work) is said to have resulted in a dangerous erosion of traditional gender roles and personality traits.

Women have supposedly become less tender and nurturant, and this is said to prevent them from adequately performing their domestic and familial functions. Men, on the other hand, are believed to have become less strong and resourceful since they no longer have a 'weaker sex' to protect. According to psychiatrist A.I. Belkin, this can lead to a feeling of 'sexlessness', which 'expresses itself in anti-social behaviour such as alcoholism, drug-taking and homosexuality'.[33]

Could this threat to patriarchal gender relations lie, then, on a subconscious level, behind the scenes of rape and violence? As already noted, there is a definite linking of phallus and weapon; *Blown Kiss* offers a particularly clear example of this. There is also a proliferation of scenes suggesting male control and ownership of women. In *Picnic on the Beach* the rapist tries at first to buy the woman from her boyfriend by offering him a tape-recorder; in *The Assassin* the first victim's punishment is not levelled at him but at his daughter, who is thus depicted as an extension of him; and in both *The Hostage* and *The Assassin* the heroines fall in love with their abusers, thus acquiescing in their own subordination. Nor, perhaps, is it accidental that the mother of the murdered child in *Satan* is in a powerful professional position, which is far from usual for women within the traditional gender divide. The murder of her child – which, as Freud would have it, functions as penis substitute – could be interpreted as a way of 'castrating' her and hence returning her to a position of female passivity. In this way, patriarchy is protected.

In short, as suggested at the outset, sex in the Russian cinema in the perestroika era is a more complex matter than it at first appears. I have tried to explore a variety of images and suggest a number of possible reasons for them. Experimentation with new images and genres is generally to be applauded. However, the proliferation of images of sexual violence against women is a disturbing new development, and not one which is likely to further the cause of women's equality. Whether it continues, in the light of the political changes currently underway, remains to be seen.

Acknowledgements

I would like to express my gratitude to Yelena Stishova of the journal *Iskusstvo kino* for inviting me to screenings at the journal's offices in July and early August 1991, and for sharing with me her own insights into contemporary Soviet cinema. I also wish to thank Savva Kulish for inviting me to see, and discuss with him, his film *Tragedy Rock-Style*. Finally, I would like to acknowledge my gratitude to the organisers of the Sixteenth and Seventeenth Moscow Film Festivals, of 1989 and 1991, for granting me accreditation.

References

1. Y. Zhenin, N. Karakoleva and D. Smirnova, 'Buying and selling', *Kino-glaz* (English version), 1991, no. 1, p. 30.
2. T. Khlopyankina, 'Vsyo razresheno?', *Iskusstvo kino*, 1989, no. 7, p. 50.
3. Irina Levi, 'Igra v kotoroi net pobeditelei', *Molodoi kommunist*, 1990, no. 4, p. 96.
4. V.I. Lenin, '*On the Emancipation of Women* (Moscow: 1972). Appendix to Clara Zetkin: 'My Recollections of Lenin', p. 101.
5. See Alexandra Kollontai, 'Make Way for Winged Eros: a Letter to Working Youth', in *Alexandra Kollontai: Selected Writings* (London: 1977), pp. 276–92.
6. See, for example, Yelena Stishova, 'Sex u nas net!', *Iskusstvo kino*, 1991, no. 6, pp. 3–4.
7. See Elizabeth Waters, 'Restructuring the "Woman Question": Perestroika and Prostitution', in *Feminist Review*, Autumn 1989, no. 33, p. 5.
8. For a rather coy mention of this game, see 'My igrali v romashku. . ' ('We Were Playing Daisy'), *Zdorovye*, 1987, no. 8, pp. 10–11.
9. See Herbert Eagle, 'The Indexality of *Little Vera* and the end of Socialist Realism', *Wide Angle*, October 1990, vol. 12, no. 4, pp. 26–37.
10. See Andrei Zorky, 'Ya so zlostyu vykrikivayu', *Sovetsky ekran*, 1989, no. 2, pp. 18–19.
11. Quoted in Andrew Wilson and Nina Bachkatova, *Living with Glasnost. Youth and Society in a Changing Russia* (Harmondsworth: 1988), p. 160.
12. Personal discussion with Savva Kulish in Moscow, August 1991.
13. Quoted by Stephen E. Deane, 'Recent Trends in Soviet Cinema', *Meeting Report of the Kennan Institute*, 1990, vol. 7, no. 11, p. 27.
14. Khlopyankina, 'Vsyo razresheno?', p. 50.
15. See 'Yeshcho odna "zakrytaya" tema', *Argumenty i fakty*, 1990, no. 16, p. 7.
16. 'Interdevochka', *Sovetsky ekran*, no. 3, 1989, p. 33.
17. Erica Sheen, 'Serial Killings', *Journal of Gender Studies*, May 1991, vol. 1, no. 1, p. 74.
18. See Galina Sillaste 'Zhenshchiny o samikh sebe', *Rabotnitsa*, November 1990, p. 7.
19. See, for example, E. Ann Kaplan, *Women and Film* (New York and London: 1983), pp. 14–15.

20. Personal discussion with Yelena Stishova, Moscow, August 1991.
21. *Stolitsa*, no. 23, July 1991.
22. Neya Zorkaya, *The Illustrated History of the Soviet Cinema* (New York: 1989), p. 252.
23. Marina Drozdova discusses this film at some length in her chapter in Lynne Attwood (ed.), *Red Women on the Silver Screen* (London: 1993).
24. Annette Kuhn, *Women's Pictures: Feminism and Cinema* (London: 1982), p. xi.
25. The same is true, according to feminist film theorists, in Western cinema. See Laura Mulvey, *Visual and Other Pleasures* (London: 1989), p. 21.
26. Kaplan, *Women and Film*, p. 6.
27. See Attwood (ed.), *Red Women on the Silver Screen*.
28. Khlopyankina, 'Vsyo razresheno?', p. 50.
29. Kaplan, *Women and Film*, p. 34.
30. Kuhn, *Women's Pictures*, p. 9.
31. See Kaplan, *Women and Film*, p. 7.
32. See Lynne Attwood, *The New Soviet Man and Woman: Sex Role Socialization in the USSR* (London and Bloomington, Ind.: 1990).
33. A.I. Belkin, 'Masculine, Feminine or Neutral?', *The UNESCO Courier* (English edn), August–September 1975, p. 61.

Filmography

This list gives English and Russian titles, the date of release (if the film was shelved for some time, the date of completion is listed first and then the date of release) and the director.

Adam's Rib (Rebro Adama) (1990), Vyacheslav Krishtofovich
The Assassin (Palach) (1990), Victor Sergeyev
The Asthenic Syndrome (Astenichesky sindrom) (1990), Kira Muratova
Blown Kiss (Vozdushny potselui) (1990), Abai Kaprykov
Brief Encounters (Korotkie vstrechi) (1968/1987), Kira Muratova
The Burn (Ozhog) (1989), Gennady Gladkov
Comrade Stalin's Trip to Africa (Puteshestvie Tovarishcha Stalina v Afriku) (1990), Irakly Kvirikadze
An Extraordinary Incident on a Regional Scale (Ch P rayonnovo masshtaba) (1989), Sergei Snezhkin
Fools Die on Fridays (Duraki umirayut po pyatnitsam) (1990), Rudolf Fruntov
High-Risk Groups (Gruppy Riska) (1988), Alexei Nikishin
The Hostage (Zolozhnitsa) (1990), Sergei Ashkenazi
How Do You Do? (Khau du yu du) (1988), Sergei Baranov
International Girl (Interdevochka) (1989), Pyotr Todorovsky

Little Vera (Malenkaya Vera) (1988), Vasily Pichul
Long Farewells (Dolgie provody) (1971/1987), Kira Muratova
Marite (1947), Vera Stroyeva
October (Oktyabr) (1928), Sergei Eisenstein
Picnic on the Beach (Diky Plyazh) (1990?), Natalya Kupakozova
Prisoner No. 217 (Chelovek No. 217) (1944), Mikhail Romm
Satan (Satana) (1990), Victor Aristov
Seven Days After Murder (Sem dnei posle ubiystvo) (1990), Robert Odzhagov
She Defends the Motherland (Ona zashchishchaet rodinu) (1943), Friedrich Ermler
Some Interviews on Personal Questions (Neskolko intervyu po lichnym voprosam) (1979), Lena Gogoberidze
To Die for Love (Umeret ot lyubvi) (1990), Tofak Shakhverdiev
Tragedy Rock-Style (Tragediya v stile rok) (1988), Savva Kulish
Zoya (1944), Lev Arnshtam

4

Sexual Minorities

IGOR KON

History

Attitudes to unusual, deviant – in the moral or sociopsychological sense – forms of sexuality, of which the most common is homosexuality, depend everywhere and always on three major factors: the general level of social toleration in society; the level of society's sexual culture and enlightenment; and the nature of its traditional culture and religion.

In that respect pre-revolutionary Russia differed little from the countries of Western Europe. In fact, attitudes to homosexuality in Ancient Rus were *more* tolerant than in medieval Europe. Sergei Solovyov, the most noted Russian historian of the nineteenth century, wrote that nowhere, neither in West nor East, were attitudes to that 'unnatural vice' so free and easy as in Russia.[1] That opinion is shared by presentday scholars.[2]

Although the Russian Orthodox Church severely condemned 'sodomy' and other forms of male and female homosexuality – it was especially perturbed about it spreading in the monasteries – it tended to turn a blind eye to such things in everyday life. In Russia homosexuality was not an 'unmentionable' subject; in fact it was often the subject of very frank discussion and ribald jokes. This state of affairs appalled many European diplomats and travellers of the sixteenth and seventeenth centuries, as witnessed in the memoirs of Sigmund von Herberstein, George Turberville and Jurai Krizhanitch.

The first state, secular laws against sodomy appeared in Russia only in the eighteenth century, during the reign of Peter the Great, in his 1706 and 1716 military statutes drawn up on the Swedish model.[3] Peter soon changed the initially instituted punishment of burning at the stake to corporal punishment, with capital punishment reserved only for rape – even that applied only to soldiers and not civilians. In the criminal code of 1832 based on the German model, Article 995 declared 'sodomy' (*muzhelozhstvo*), or 'anal contact', to be punishable by deprivation of all rights and exile to Siberia for between four and five years; rape or seduction of a minor was to be punished by hard labour for between ten and 20 years. The new criminal legislation adopted in 1903 modified these punishments. Under Article 516, sodomy was punishable by incarceration for no less than three months or, given aggravating circumstances, for between three and eight years.

This legislation, however, was employed extremely rarely. Many Russian aristocrats, including members of the imperial family, as well as eminent artistic figures of the turn of the century openly led a homo- or bisexual way of life – such people as the Grand Duke Sergei Alexandrovich, the conservative publicist and publisher Prince Vladimir Meshchersky, the poet Alexei Apukhtin, the composer Pyotr Tchaikovsky,[4] the theatrical impresario Sergei Diaghilev, the writers Dmitri Filosofov and Konstantin Leontiev, and the traveller Nikolai Przhevalsky. There were also quite a few well-known lesbian couples. Russian homoerotic poetry, literature and painting began to appear in the early years of the century (the works of Mikhail Kuzmin, Nikolai Klyuev and Lidiya Zinovieva-Annibal, for instance). The issue of same-sex love began to be debated seriously and sympathetically in philosophical, scientific and artistic literature (as, for example, in the work of Vasily Rozanov). One of the founders of the Cadet Party, the lawyer Vladimir Nabokov, father of the celebrated writer, published an article in 1903 on the legal status of homosexuals in Russia.[5]

After the February 1917 Revolution, two completely different political parties – the Anarchists and the Cadets – officially proposed revoking anti-homosexual legislation. The Bolsheviks as a party had no well-defined position on the issue. In his book *The Origin of the Family, Private Property and the State*, Friedrich Engels had calmly and dispassionately written of Ancient Greek love for boys, yet in a letter to Marx in 1869 he dismisses writings on homosexuality by Karl Ulrichs in a disparaging and totally unsympathetic way.[6] August Bebel, along with other German intellectuals of the time, signed an appeal to have homosexuality decriminalised. Lenin, on the other hand, was always circumspect in regard to sex in any form.

Never the less, with the demise of the old criminal code in the

Russian Federation, the legal persecution of homosexuals ceased. In the Russian Criminal Code of 1922 and 1926, homosexuality is not referred to at all, but in those parts of the old Russian Empire where it was most widespread – the Islamic republics of Azerbaidzhan, Turkmenia and Uzbekistan, as well as in Christian Georgia – the legislation remained in force.

The official stance of Soviet medicine and law in the 1920s tended to treat homosexuality as a sickness rather than a crime. In 1930 Mark Sereisky wrote in the *Great Soviet Encyclopaedia*,

> Soviet legislation does not recognise so-called crimes against morality. Our legislation proceeds from the principle of protecting society and therefore countenances punishment only in those instances when young and under-age children are the object of homosexual interest . . . While recognising the incorrectness of homosexual development, society does not and cannot put the blame for it on those who bear those traits . . . While emphasising the importance of the causes that give rise to such an anomaly, our society combines therapeutic and sanitary measures with all the necessary conditions to enable homosexuals to live as trouble-free a life as possible and to resolve their problems of estrangement from society within the new collective.[7]

Sereisky hoped that a 'radical cure' for all homosexuals could be found by transplanting the testicles of heterosexual men onto homosexuals.

Up to the 1930s the situation of Soviet homosexuals, who frequently called themselves 'blues',[8] was reasonably bearable and many played a prominent part in Soviet culture (Karlinsky mentions the Foreign Affairs Commissar Georgi Chicherin, the poets Mikhail Kuzmin, Nikolai Klyuev and Sofia Parnak, and the film director Sergei Eisenstein. Bisexuals evidently included Sergei Yesenin, Marina Tsvetaeva and Ryurik Ivnen).[9] However, the opportunity for an open, philosophical and artistic discussion of the theme, which had begun in the early part of the century, gradually diminished. Then, on 17 December 1933, the All-Union Central Executive Committee issued a resolution which became law on 7 March 1934; this once again made 'sodomy' a criminal offence in all Soviet republics. In line with Article 121 of the Russian Federation Criminal Code, it is punishable by deprivation of freedom for a term of up to five years – or for up to eight years in the event of the use of physical violence or the threat of violence, or in relation to a minor, or if it involves abuse of the victim's dependent position.

Why such a law was adopted precisely at that time is not exactly known, but it was in full accord with the overall repressive spirit of the Stalin era.

It is sad to note here the lack of principle displayed by the great Russian writer Maxim Gorky on the issue of homosexuality. In 1927 he published a sympathetic foreword to the Russian translation of Stefan Zweig's *Confused Feelings*, in which he was full of praise for the writer in exposing yet another human tragedy.[10] In 1934, however, Gorky had an article printed in both *Pravda* and *Izvestiya* welcoming the new repressive legislation; it was 'a triumph of proletarian humanism'. He even maintained that legalisation of homosexuality was one reason for the victory of German fascism. And this was said at a time when the fascists were shooting German homosexuals, branded as the 'communist plague'.[11].

In January 1936 Nikolai Krylenko, People's Commissar for Justice, announced that homosexuality was a product of the decadence of the exploiting classes; in a socialist society based on healthy principles, such people, in Krylenko's words, should have no place. Homosexuality was therefore directly 'connected' with counterrevolution.[12] Somewhat later Soviet lawyers talked of homosexuality primarily as a manifestation of the 'moral decadence of the bourgeoisie', reiterating verbatim the arguments of German fascists.

Nobody knows what was the total number of casualties of this inhuman legislation. According to S.P. Shcherbakov, an average of 1000 men went before the courts every year. The only official information on the subject came to light after the start of perestroika: in 1987 as many as 831 men were sentenced under this law. One would imagine that victims in previous years were much more numerous. According to unofficial figures, the Prosecutor's Office dealt with about 1,000 cases each year after 1987, though most did not reach the courts. However, the situation once more took a turn for the worse in 1991.

On 7 May 1991 the local court in Moscow's Volgograd District sentenced a certain V. Mironov to three years' deprivation of freedom under Article 121.1 for an incident alleged to have taken place in 1988. Mironov and his partner were both over 40 years of age. The only grounds for conviction were the testimony of witnesses who actually withdrew their statements in court, claiming that they had given them under duress. In so far as Mironov had been in custody since 11 October 1990, one may conjecture that the prosecution needed 'forced' evidence to justify the long preliminary incarceration. Such things used to happen fairly frequently in the USSR. An additional, though again illegal, piece of evidence against Mironov was that he had been convicted under the same Article several years before – although the conviction had long since been expunged. If such kangaroo courts could be held in Moscow, it is not hard to imagine what went on in the provinces.

Article 121 applied not only to homosexuals; it was frequently used up till the 1980s against dissidents and to extend terms in labour camps. Sometimes the evil hand of the KGB was patently obvious in such cases. That happened, for example, in the early 1980s with the eminent Leningrad archeologist Lev Klein, whose case was conducted from start to finish by the local KGB in crude violation of all procedural norms. The point of such cases was to cow intellectuals into meek submission.

Application of the law has always been selective. As long as they did not fall foul of the authorities, certain homosexual cultural and artistic celebrities enjoyed relative immunity. Once they overstepped the mark, however, the law descended upon them with a vengeance. That was what brought down the great Armenian film producer Sergei Paradzhanov; even today the Kiev prosecutor is still boasting of his handiwork there.[13] Another victim in the latter part of the 1980s was Zinovy Korogodsky, Chief Director of the Leningrad Yuny Zritel Theatre; he was arraigned before a court, sacked from his job and deprived of his titles. Such examples are legion.

Glasnost and Homosexuality

The initial anti-homosexual campaign in the Soviet press was short-lived. By the mid-1930s a complete and utter silence had fallen over the entire issue. Homosexuality was simply never mentioned anywhere; it became 'the unmentionable sin' in the literal sense of the words. The conspiracy of silence extended even to such well-known topics as phallic cults or pederasty in ancient societies. In 1974 I submitted an article on 'The Concept of Friendship in Ancient Greece' for publication in a specialist magazine on ancient history.[14] Naturally, every member of the editorial board knew full well what Greek pederasty was. Yet two academic women demanded that the word should be totally eradicated from the article. Finally, on the advice of the editor-in-chief, S.L. Utchenko, who had staunchly supported my article, it was published with the euphemism 'those specific relationships'. In ordinary periodicals, there could be no mention at all of 'that', even through the gentlest of hints.[15] This silence further intensified the tragedy of Soviet 'blues': not only did they fear persecution and blackmail, they could not even develop an adequate self-awareness and comprehend exactly who they were.

Medicine also had little comfort for gays. Up to the 1970s Soviet sexology barely existed, and when the odd book on sexopathology began to appear, homosexuality was treated as a pernicious 'sexual perversion', a disease that had to be treated.[16] Even the most liberal and enlightened Soviet sexopathologists and psychiatrists – with very rare exceptions – to this day regard homosexuality as a disease and reproduce in their books innumerable stupidities and negative stereotypes typical of the mass psyche. In a most recent guide to sexopathology,[17] homosexuality is defined as a 'pathological orientation' and is discussed in purely biological terms. Apart from biological causes, the authors state that 'strong pathogenic factors encouraging the formation of homosexual orientations may be parents and teachers who encourage a hostile attitude to the opposite sex.'[18]

It is hardly surprising that Soviet 'blues' eagerly latched on to any crumbs of more or less trustworthy information on their problems. With enormous difficulty and risk to themselves, they sometimes obtained old works of Freud and foreign literature. When there appeared a short and dispassionate article on teenage gayness in a narrowly specialist, limited-circulation book, absolutely unattainable by the ordinary reader, it was immediately photocopied and distributed far and wide.[19]

In the early 1980s a campaign against homosexuality was launched in educational literature. In a teaching aid written by A. Khripkova and D. Kolesov and printed in no less than a million copies, homosexuality was described as a dangerous pathology and an 'infringement of normal sexual relations'.

> Homosexuality goes against both normal heterosexual relations and the whole set of cultural and moral achievements of our society. For that reason it merits censure both as a social phenomenon and as a cast of mind and human conduct . . . Anti-homosexual therapy is a vital component of the sexual hygiene of boys and adolescents [the physiologist authors evidently know

nothing of female homosexuality]. We must stop any influence from factors that may dispose boys and adolescents against the female sex; we must control the nature of their relationships with members of their own sex and we must be circumspect in our choice of staff for educational institutions like boarding schools.[20]

Evidently not only police and medical personnel, but schoolteachers as well had to be on their guard.

The AIDS epidemic worsened matters for homosexuals. When the virus was just being identified in the US, the first information in the Soviet press went roughly as follows: an unknown disease has just hit America; its victims are homosexuals, drug addicts and Puerto Ricans. Brought up in the spirit of internationalism, Soviet citizens found it hard to understand why this illness should affect Puerto Ricans. Homosexuals and drug addicts, fair enough – God is punishing them for their sins – but why on earth Puerto Ricans? Surely God isn't a racist!

Subsequently things became even worse. In 1986 Medical Academician Nikolai Burgasov, onetime Deputy Health Minister and Chief Hygiene Doctor of the USSR, went on record as saying that Soviet people had nothing to fear from AIDS in so far as homosexuality was a criminal offence, as was drug addiction.[21] Somewhat later, A. Potapov, the former Russian Federation Health Minister, while discussing drug addiction in the weekly *Literaturnaya gazeta*, not only connected the problem with homosexuality but even related a story that a frenzied mob had recently lynched a couple of gay men in Paris. He claimed that the porno-business was on the wane in Western Europe and he concluded with 'You see how human decency is ringing the changes . . .'[22] And no one even remarked on the abomination of his words.

When AIDS did arrive in the USSR, the two men in charge of the state epidemiology programme, Valentin Pokrovsky (then President of the USSR Academy of Medical Sciences) and his son Vadim, largely referred in their public statements to morality and the so-called risk groups, especially gays, portraying them as carriers not only of the dreaded virus but of just about every other vice. Those were their sincere convictions, for homosexuality had never been officially heard of in Soviet medical colleges.

Even the liberal weekly *Ogonyok* wrote with undisguised revulsion and condemnation when it published its first article on AIDS patients and the first Soviet person to fall victim to the terrible disease, a gay engineer who had contracted the virus in Africa. This hypocritical moralising and the search for scapegoats instead of a real socio-hygienic policy was first challenged in 1988 in an interview with me in the same journal.[23] It has to be said that glasnost in combination with the AIDS threat made it possible to have a more or less frank discussion of sexual orientations in both popular and scholarly literature.

In a textbook on the psychohygiene of sex in children, for instance, published for doctors in 1986, the section 'Formation of Sexual Orientations' contains information on adolescent homosexuality examined as an aspect of normal psychosexual development, rather than as a 'sexual perversion'.[24] Moreover, the first and only Soviet book on general sex issues, published in 1988 with a print run of 550,000, has a chapter on sexual orientations which sets out contemporary theories, cites biological-medical, historical-anthropological and psychological statistics and demonstrates the erroneous and damaging nature of discrimination against homosexuals.[25] But the book skirts specific issues relating to gays in the USSR and all the juridical questions surrounding them. The question of whether homosexuality is a lifestyle or an illness is presented as controversial. Without the occasional silence and compromise the book would not have been published by a medical, let alone any other, Soviet publishing house. As it is, *the book was unpublished for ten years.*

In the third edition of the only Soviet textbook on juvenile psychology for teachers and parents in 60 years (of which 800,000 copies were printed), a few pages appeared on adolescent homosexuality which, by contrast with the work of A. Khripkova and D. Kolesov, was presented as a variant of normal psychosexual development rather than as a disease or consequence of a young lad being perverted by adults; it stressed that 'intimate erotic feelings of adolescents lie beyond the scope of pedagogical control' and that tactless intervention by adults may cause an adolescent irreparable harm. 'Human problems always lie behind sexual problems'.[26] This theme could not be aired in the book's previous editions of 1979, 1980 and 1982.

Since 1987 the popular press, particularly youth papers (*Moskovsky komsomolets, Komsomolskaya pravda, Sobesednik, Molodoi kommunist*) and periodicals like *Literaturnaya gazeta, Ogonyok, Argumenty i fakty, Yunost, Info-SPID*, the teenage magazine *Parus* and some local papers as well as radio and TV, are discussing homosexuality: What is it? How should one relate to 'blues'? Should they be treated as sick and criminal or as victims of fate? Although the publications are quite disparate in their level and content (some are semi-literate and sensation-mongering), their appearance has had a huge significance. From journalistic articles and letters from gay men and lesbians and their parents, ordinary Soviet people have for the first time come to recognise the scarred destinies, the police cruelty, the legal repression, the sexual violence in prison, labour camp and armed forces and, finally, the tragic, inescapable loneliness experienced by people living in constant fear and unable to meet any of their own sort. Each publication has provoked a whole stream of contradictory responses which the newspaper editors have just not known how to handle.

The paramount issue is the decriminalisation of homosexuality. Back in 1973, the Leningrad lawyers Mikhail Shargorodsky and Pavel Osipov maintained in their criminal law textbook that Soviet legal literature had never contained any logical or scientific arguments in favour of criminalising contacts between mutually consenting adult men; they also revealed that some other socialist countries had revoked such laws.[27] Decriminalisation has long been the subject of debate in professional circles. Professor Alexei Ignatov, the leading Soviet legal authority on 'sex crimes', raised the issue before the senior levels of the USSR Ministry of Internal Affairs back in 1979. With the backing of medical professors Georgi Vasilchenko and Dmitri Isayev, I tried to publish an article on the theme in the legal journal *Sovetskoye gosudarstvo i pravo* as long ago as 1982. All in vain.

A whole series of arguments have been adduced in favour of decriminalisation:

- Soviet legislation was out of step with international law;
- it conflicted with the general conclusions of presentday science;
- humanitarian considerations: people should be free to choose their sexual preference;
- the lack of internal logic in the legal system itself in punishing only male homosexuality;
- the social damage brought about through alienating gays from society and forcing them underground;
- sanitary-hygienic considerations, the difficulties of combating VD and, now, AIDS;
- the inevitable abuses by law and order agencies when applying such legislation.

Although the arguments did not spill over into the newspapers, Article 121 was excluded from the draft new Russian Federation Criminal Code prepared by a law-making commission as far back as in the mid-1980s. However, at the time of writing (late 1992) discussion and adoption of the new code were being delayed for a number of reasons, while Article 121 was being debated on TV and in the papers.

Generally speaking three points of view predominate:

1. Fully to revoke Article 121 and to remove any mention of sexual preferences from the criminal legislation, in as much as children and adolescents are protected, irrespective of their sex, by other articles. This was a position held by lawyers like Alexei Ignatov and Alexander Yakovlev, the sociologist Igor Kon, the psycho-endocrinologist Aron Belkin and various other professional people.
2. To revoke criminal responsibility for homosexual contacts between consenting adults, but to maintain the second part of the Article concerning children and minors. This was a position held by many officials of the Internal Affairs Ministry[28] and some gay and lesbian activists.
3. To leave everything as it was. This was the demand of right-wing nationalists and religious organisations.

While arguments in the media continue to rage, Soviet 'blues' remain just as oppressed and defenceless as ever.

In early 1992, a special issue of the journal *Zakon* (supplement to *Izvestiya*) published the draft of the new Russian Criminal Code. It omitted the old Article 121 but included a new Article 132, 'Buggery or Gratification of Sexual Passion in Other Perverted Forms'. According to this Article,

buggery, lesbianism or gratification of sexual passion [one version says 'sexual needs'] in other perverted forms, carried out with the use of physical force or threat thereof, or by exploiting the helpless state of the victim, shall be punished by restriction on freedom for up to three years or deprivation of freedom from two to three years.

Repeat offences, or the same actions committed by persons guilty of rape, or committed by a group, would be punished by deprivation of freedom for a period of between five and seven years; in the event of serious consequences for the victim, or if the victim was known by the guilty party to have been a minor (under 14 years of age), the penalty would be loss of freedom for between seven and twelve years.

This text is palpably contradictory. On the one hand, it says that homosexual relations between consulting adults are no longer punishable; the law is no longer regulating sexual behaviour, simply protecting the individual from sexual assault. On the other, it continues to regard homosexuality as a 'perversion', and now with the addition of lesbianism, which was not included in any previous legislation. This proposal is clearly a step backwards.

The concept of 'perverted forms' is confusing. Evidently, it refers not only to buggery but to other means of anal and oral penetration. It is interesting that under this Article these would not be regarded as rape and would be punishable, given aggravating circumstances, more leniently than straightforward rape.

It should be emphasised that, as of mid-1992, this is still a *draft* and the major battle lies ahead. Very many people both in the Russian Parliament and outside it are active opponents of decriminalising homosexuality.

Victims Fight Back

Soviet society generally was extremely intolerant of any dissidence and uncommon behaviour, even the most innocent. Homosexuals were indeed the most stigmatised social group in the USSR. According to statistics of the All-Union Public Opinion Centre issued in November 1989 (based on a representative sample of 2,600 people), the question of 'How ought one to deal with homosexuals?' was answered as follows: 33 per cent were for 'eliminating' them; 30 per cent for 'isolating them from society'; 10 per cent for 'leaving them to themselves'; and only 6 per cent for 'helping them'.[29]

Homophobia expressed in this survey strongly depended on people's level of education ('eliminating' homosexuals was the view held by 38 per cent of people with incomplete secondary education, but only 22 per cent of those with higher education) and on age (the most 'intolerant' were people over 50 years of age), and is practically unrelated to gender. In social background, the most homophobic people fell into three groups – pensioners, housewives and members of the armed forces – while the least homophobic were members of cooperatives (0 per cent for 'elimination' and 5 per cent for 'help') and scholars and artists (0 per cent for 'elimination', although 34 per cent for 'isolation'). There was no correlation between homophobic feelings and property status, but there was a certain cultural factor: the people who kept a large number of books at home appeared to be considerably more liberal than those who did not. Regionally, homophobia was strongest in Uzbekistan (54 per cent for 'elimination'), and then in Georgia and Armenia in the Caucasus (43 per cent), with the most liberal areas being Moscow and Lithuania (26 per cent). As for religious affiliation, Muslims were far less tolerant than Christians. Much also depended on the density of one's residential area: Muscovites were sexually more tolerant than residents of peripheral towns and rural dwellers. All this, of course, is only the most general and superficial information. The sociologists conducting the survey were interested more in the overall level of social toleration than in homophobia itself.

None the less, we can take as proven that the attitude towards homosexuals in the USSR was substantially worse than towards any other negatively evaluated social group, even prostitutes and drug addicts with whom, thanks to the tendentious anti-AIDS propaganda, homosexuality was frequently associated. Homophobia was deliberately fomented and spread by right-wing chauvinistic media like the Russian Communist Party daily *Sovetskaya Rossiya*, the literary magazines *Nash sovremennik* and *Molodaya gvardia*, the weekly of the USSR Internal Affairs Ministry *Shchit i mech*, and Alexander Nevzorov's Leningrad TV programme '600 Seconds'.

Such sentiments found some support among scholars as well. For example, Valentin Pokrovsky, President of the USSR Academy of Medical Sciences, who headed the state anti-AIDS programmes, pronounced in an interview given to the newspaper *Megapolis-express* that AIDS was 'a moral sickness'; he branded as absurd 'demands to legalise homosexuality'. To the journalist's question as to whether it could really be regarded as a disease, the learned professor replied,

It is precisely a disease. There are people who are genetically orientated on that type of sexual contact. It is frankly absurd to regard that as normal. It is even more absurd to regard as normal healthy people who impose homosexual relations on and corrupt minors because of their excess of sexual passion. It is not so much a disease as depravity that has to be combated, precisely by legal means.[30]

The unholy alliance of medics and prejudiced police and lawyers has deprived sexual minorities of all rights and protection in medical as well as social and legal terms. Soviet legislation on measures to combat AIDS and the USSR Health Ministry directive on the subject were so vague as to make anyone liable to prosecution for homosexuality, evidence or no evidence, and therefore liable to forcible AIDS-testing and other offensive measures. But this issue is not just one of criminal sanctions.

Gay men and lesbians have had nowhere to meet or mix with people like themselves. The big cities naturally have well-known gay meeting places. But fear of exposure has made most contacts impersonal, anonymous – 'one-night-stands' deprived of human warmth and psychological intimacy. That is what the majority of 'blues' complain about.

Extensive and impersonal sex sharply increases the risk of infection from VD or AIDS. According to statistics from Ukrainian and Belorussian venereological centres, gay men constitute in excess of 30 per cent of all syphilis patients; in Latvia they comprise more than half. Afraid of exposure, homosexuals rarely seek medical advice; if they do it is often too late. In Moscow, 84 per cent of late hospitalisation cases of syphilis involve gay men. This makes it even more difficult to locate the source of the infection. According to a Moscow specialist in venereal diseases, Professor Konstantin Borisenko, Director-General of the Sexually Transmitted Diseases Prevention Association, the percentage of known sources for syphilis infection among gay men is no higher than 7.5–10 per cent, while for other groups it is about 50–70 per cent.[31] That is why Borisenko, by contrast with his colleague Pokrovsky, is an ardent campaigner for the decriminalisation of homosexuality, since he realises that without that it will be impossible to improve the epidemiological situation.

Street toilet contacts are dangerous in other respects. Organised gangs of thugs, sometimes with the covert backing of the police, provoke, blackmail, mug, viciously beat up and even murder 'blues'. In doing so they proclaim themselves protectors of public morality, referring to their actions as 'repairs' (*remont*) that is, righting wrongs. As most gay men are afraid of reporting such incidents to the police, most crimes against them go unpunished – and then the police blame them for being breeding-grounds of crime. Murder for robbery is time and again portrayed as the result of a pathological jealousy peculiar to homosexuals.

Gay men in confinement have to endure absolutely unbearable conditions. A person who ended up in prison or labour camp under Article 121 usually became straightaway a 'no-rights odd-bod' and recipient of constant taunts and persecution from other prisoners. Further, the rape of adolescents and young men is widespread in both gaols and labour camps; after such assaults the victims forfeit all human rights, become 'degraded' and have to act submissively to their violators. The status of the 'degraded' is even worse than that of voluntarily passive homosexuals who, to a certain degree, select their own partners and protectors (who perform an active, 'male' sexual role that is not stigmatised and is even encouraged). The 'degraded', on the other hand, are fair game for anyone. (It is interesting that some Russian medical experts still make a 'fundamental' division of homosexuals into 'active' and 'passive' depending on preferred sexual positions; moreover, they associate 'passive' with 'inborn' and 'genuine', and 'active' with 'acquired' homosexuality.)

Prison sexual symbolism and rituals are more or less universal.[32] But day-to-day life depends on the nature of the camp. In the 'red' camp, where power resides with the administration, the inmates may still find some sort of protection. In the 'black' camps, however, where it is actually the criminals who run things, such people are utterly defenceless. The staff of the prison or labour camp is effectively powerless to alter these relations; sometimes they even use them in their own interests. One informer, a young man enlisted by the KGB, tells how, when he reported a case of rape to his superior, the man told him:

Sasha, what difference does it make? They're all the same to us, but it's better when we have more people raped, since they're more likely to contact the administration and work their butts off; after all, they've nothing left to do than drown themselves in work and seek our help against the 'wolves' . . . So I say, to hell with them, with the 'cocks' . . .[33]

Generally speaking, the mores of Soviet prisons and the rituals adopted in them, the language and symbols, differ little from those of American or other similar institutions.[34] On the other hand, Soviet prisons are much less comfortable than those in the West, so everything is even more vicious and sordid. It is from here, from the criminal subculture which has permeated all aspects of life in Soviet society, that corresponding mores have spread to the armed forces. The bullying (*dedovshchina*), that tyrannical power of the 'old sweats' over the new recruits, very frequently involves overt or covert elements of homosexual abuse. In recent years the army itself has begun to recognise its existence.

When talking of homosexuality, Russians almost always mean male homosexuality; the press has only recently started to mention lesbianism.[35] All the same, life for lesbians is no better. It is true that their relationships do not come under any article in the criminal code, and intimacy between women is less remarkable to the surrounding world. On the other hand, a young girl in our society who is aware of her psychosexual difference finds it harder than a man to find a close relationship. And society's attitude is just as obdurate: ridicule, persecution, expulsion from college or work, threats to take her children away. The idea that homosexuals, men or women, can actually be good parents would be absolutely anathema to virtually everyone in the former USSR.

The old Soviet Union has other sexual minorities of course: paedophiles, zoophilists, sadomasochists, transvestites and trans- sexuals. Their problems are seen exclusively in medical terms, as 'sexual perversions' or 'violations of sexual self-awareness (auto- identification)'.[36] The psycho-endocrinologist Professor Aron Belkin began research back in the 1970s on gender transpositions and clinical transsexualism. But the psychological and social aspects of the problem are not explored and are rarely taken into consideration. Gender transposition is frequently depicted in the popular press in an extremely simplified form, while transvestites and transsexualism are seen by the ordinary observer as odd and exotic, belonging to the realm of compulsory medical correction or elimination. Nobody anywhere discusses the issue of their human and civil rights. So the problem of sexual minorities is reduced to that of gay men and lesbians.

Up to the end of the 1980s Soviet 'blues' were merely victims who could only complain about their fate and make futile entreaties regarding their humiliation. It has to be said that rare exceptions did exist. In 1984 some 30 young people in Leningrad led by Alexander Zaremba came together to form a gay and lesbian group and a 'gay laboratory'; they established contact with a Finnish gay and lesbian association, sent information to the West about the appalling status of Soviet 'blues' and, as much as they were able to, began to undertake therapeutic work on the AIDS issue, something that Soviet medicine had failed to do. Immediately, however, the group came under KGB surveillance followed by political and ideological accusation, threats and repression, as a result of which some were browbeaten into emigration, others into silence.

During the initial glasnost years the 'experts' were the only ones to talk about sexual minority problems, in tones of strained sympathy. Steadily, however, 'blues' themselves ventured into print: the victims took on the mantle of fighters. Western gay organisations and periodicals rendered considerable service in promoting their self-awareness.

The first international conference to be held on Soviet territory on sexual minorities and changing attitudes to homosexuality in twentieth-century Europe took place on 28–30 May 1990 in the Estonian capital of Tallinn, on the initiative of the Estonian Academy of Sciences History Institute and with the backing of several Western gay communities. Many eminent overseas scholars took part in the conference; they included Geoffrey Weeks and Gert Hekma. Although the Soviet contributions, apart from the Estonian, fell short of the professional level of the Western, the conference generally was a success and helped to raise the self-esteem and enhance the social and psychological identity of Soviet gays and lesbians. The first international scholarly contacts had been made.

Within the framework of the Soviet–Finnish programme for studying social minorities, directed from Tallinn by the demographer Teet Veispak, the first comparative research is being undertaken into the position and problems of sexual minorities in Estonia and Finland. Its questionnaires are steadily making their way into Russia as well.

Gay Associations: Teething Troubles

The first Sexual Minority Association (Alliance of Lesbians and Homosexuals) came into being in Moscow in late 1989. Its programme emphasised that it was 'primarily a legal defence organisation with its principal goal as the attainment of complete equality before the law for people of different sexual preferences'. The Association's key tasks were to campaign to revoke Article 121.1 (criminal prosection for homosexual acts between consenting male adults); to change public attitudes (or, more exactly, prejudices) towards sexual minorities, employing every possible means through the official media; to organise the social rehabilitation of AIDS patients; to publish the newspaper *Tema* (*The Theme*) and other material; to help people to locate friends and like-minded acquaintances. The Association considered it important to study homosexual problems, to campaign for safe sex and to collect all available information on the persecution of homosexuals. For the moment it had no formal membership; anyone over the age of 18 could join.

The newspaper *SPID-info* published the Association's appeal to the USSR President and presidents of the USSR Supreme Soviet and union republics; the appeal was signed by the Association's leading activists Vladislav Ortanov, Konstantin Yevgeniev and Alexander Zubov. It also called for the revoking of discriminatory articles in the criminal code concerning consensual contacts between adults and for an amnesty for those already sentenced under those articles. At the same time the Association announced its

> unreserved condemnation of any attempts to corrupt minors and to use violence in whatever form, in regard to people of any sex and no matter by whom such attempts are made. WE ARE NOT SEEKING TO CONVERT ANYONE TO OUR BELIEFS. WE ARE WHAT NATURE MADE US. Help us to allay our fears. We are part of your lives and your spiritual community. That is not by your or our choice.[37]

Unfortunately, the political climate of Soviet society and the futility of a constructive dialogue with the authorities encouraged extremism in all social movements. Immediately after the publication of the second trial issue of *Tema*, the Association split. The signatories to the first declaration left and the Association effectively ceased to exist. The Moscow Gay and Lesbian Alliance took over, headed by Yevgeniya Debryanskaya, who had been excluded from the Democratic Union; 24 year-old Roman Kalinin became the sole publisher and editor-in-chief of *Tema*, which was officially registered with the Moscow City Council in October 1990.

The establishment of the Alliance and the official registration of *Tema* opened the way for greater opportunities for 'blues'. This was triumphantly acclaimed in the West. The fact that courageous people had stood up and openly advocated civil rights instead of mercy was an important moral initiative. But with what means was the battle to

be taken forward? The Alliance leaders, having secured political and
financial backing from American gay organisations, decided to go
ahead with street rallies and protest demonstrations under trenchant
political slogans aimed less at the domestic public than at Western
journalists. Such tactics had some success in the West.

Kalinin met considerable acclaim in the US. He was officially
received by the then Mayor of San Francisco, who declared the date
of his visit to the city 'Roman Kalinin Day'; he was granted the
freedom of the city and gained promises of free condoms to be
shipped to the USSR.[38] Fundraising efforts were undertaken in the
US to hold an international symposium in Moscow and Leningrad,
and a gay parade in Moscow under the slogan 'Turn Red Squares into
Pink Triangles' was planned.[39]

Within Russia, Kalinin's activities, in our view, have been less
successful. Soviet people may have differed in their attitudes to
Gorbachov, but Kalinin's interview in the paper *Sex-bespredel*
(*Unlimited Sex*), entitled 'I Would Not Want to Sleep with Mikhail
Gorbachov' evoked only concerted indignation. Demands by the
Libertarian Party, of which the Alliance is a member, to legalise
homosexuality, prostitution and drug addiction merit serious discussion on each separate item; but to lump them all together without
distinction – only undifferentiated slogans appear in the press –
merely reinforces the common stereotype that homosexuality, prostitution and drug addiction are one and the same and that 'such people'
deserve no leniency whatsoever. This attitude is reinforced when
'such people' manifestly demonstrate their aggression and lack of
respect for the rest of the community.

An interview with Kalinin appeared in a Moscow regional newspaper in the autumn of 1990; in it he stated that the Alliance
defended paedophiles, zoophilists and necrophiles as well as homosexuals and lesbians:

'I'm not involved with children myself, but the Alliance's position
is clear: we want the article on corruption of minors taken out of
the criminal code. We are opposed to violence, but if it does take
place by mutual consent, this is normal at any age, in any
combination of the sexes. Where do they get the children from?
They have their own channels: a child costs between three and five
thousand. The paedophile gets the enjoyment he seeks, after all a
young child has a beautiful body and soul, it doesn't do anyone any
harm . . .'

'What about dead bodies for necrophiles?'

'No problem either; you get necrophiles working in morgues, in the ambulance service, at cemeteries. Others come to an arrangement with them.'[40]

It is hard to say whether everything was said exactly as reported, but the sensationalism published by the previously unknown *Karetny ryad* was immediately picked up by TASS and the entire Party and right-wing press – *Pravda, Sovetskaya Rossiya, Semya* and many other publications, as well as the TV programme '600 Seconds'. A propaganda campaign was directed at the democratic Moscow City Council which was virulently accused of encouraging sexual perversion and pornography because it had registered *Tema* as a bona fide paper. A number of factories and offices far beyond Moscow's confines organised protest meetings, adopted resolutions with demands for immediate new elections to the Council and, at the very least, an absolute ban on *Tema* and the Gay and Lesbian Alliance. Parents were up in arms: the crime rate was rising fast, making it dangerous for children to go out alone, and now there was open defence of paedophiles and a child sex trade.

The democratic press rightly saw this as a calculated political provocation. A newspaper war raged. Moscow City Council (and not Kalinin, as the Western gay press wrote) took *Karetny ryad* to court to prove that the *Tema* programme submitted for registration to the Council contained no 'pornographic' material (nor did the issues printed before registration), and that the Council had never registered the Alliance as such. The court upheld the Council's claims and forced *Karetny ryad* to publish an apology. *Pravda*, too, afraid of a follow-up court case, apologised, though reiterating its attacks on 'sexual minorities'.[41] On this occasion Moscow City Council successfully defended its honour.

But the moral damage inflicted on sexual minorities by scandal certainly did not help. In the course of the press wrangling, both sides tried to distance themselves from 'sexual minorities'. The communist press accused the Moscow Council of conniving with them, while the City Council claimed it was the right-wing papers that advertised homosexuality by creating all the fuss. Only one influential paper, *Argumenty i fakty*, published an article demonstrating the principled legality, correctness and necessity of the legal existence of such associations, despite possible extremist outbursts typical of Soviet political affairs.[42] But what is a single temperate article in an ocean of hostility? What effect did it have on people already perturbed by events?

Roman Kalinin's political 'happenings' continued. In an item entitled 'The Next President Could be Gay', the newspaper *Kommersant* reported that Roman Kalinin, 'who was a miner in the Kuzbas for five years and has a police record of drunkenness and drug abuse'[43] was to be Russian presidential candidate for the Libertarian Party. Was this yet another newspaper canard?

There followed an interview in *Literaturnaya gazeta*, reporting that 'Roman Kalinin, leader of the Libertarian Party and Gay and Lesbian Alliance', had confirmed his presidential candidacy, saying that his major task was 'to crush the blood-suckers on the body politic – the CPSU, KGB and armed forces – as quickly as possible'.[44] The so-called presidential candidate's programme made no mention of homosexuality, although it did talk of revoking Article 121 of the Russian Federation Criminal Code (the great majority of Russians would have no idea what that Article signified). In fact, there could be no legal basis for Kalinin's presidential candidacy since he did not meet the age requirements.

If Kalinin's purpose was to court popularity at any price, he certainly achieved that. Yet one is bound to ask whether such notoriety actually improves the status and reputation of gay men and lesbians, and helps them to gain political allies in the fight for civil rights. More moderate leaders of the gay movement (Vladislav Ortanov, Olga Zhuk, Alexander Kukharsky) have roundly condemned Kalinin's antics and are endeavouring to set up their own association with a more constructive programme. But it is much more difficult to do so now since local councils have had their fingers badly burned by the *Tema* scandal.

The 'Neva Shores' (*Nevskie berega*) Gay and Lesbian Association came into being in Leningrad in October 1990 under the chairmanship of Professor Alexander Kukharsky; it proclaimed its aims as to campaign by all legal means to revoke Article 121 of the Russian Federation Criminal Code, to educate the public in a spirit of anti-homophobia, to combat sexual abuse and blackmail, to disseminate reliable information on homosexuality and to establish a gay infrastructure, including bars, clubs, discos, newspapers and libraries. The Association has the backing of the Leningrad Health Centre, and its constitution met no objections from the legal board of the Leningrad City Executive Committee. None the less, on the insistence of D.M. Veryovkin, the Leningrad Prosecutor-General, the Leningrad

Council Executive Committee Presidium declined to register it on 10 December 1990. The Oktyabrsky District Court also refused the Association permission on 20 February 1991 to appeal to the Leningrad Council; one of the 'reasons' given was the provocative nature of Kalinin's publications, which Leningraders officially condemn in no uncertain terms. The City Court also turned down the Association lawyer's protest on the affair. Even earlier, Leningrad City Council had refused to register a lesbian group, the Tchaikovsky Cultural Foundation.

The Association for Equal Rights for Homosexuals (ARGO) was established in Moscow in October 1990 and in 1991 published two trial issues of its journal *RISK* (*R*avenstvo. *I*skrennost. *S*voboda. *K*ompromiss – Equality. Sincerity. Freedom. Compromise) with Vladislav Ortanov as editor-in-chief. Meanwhile, an independent organisation for defending the rights of sexual minorities also came into being in 1991 in Latvia; while the Siberian city of Barnaul saw the first issue of a newspaper for gays and lesbians in the same year – although the editorial board immediately broke up over internal wrangles.

Practical assistance to gay men and lesbians has come from the group studying sexual minority problems attached to the Moscow company Medicine and Reproduction (Meditsina i reproduktsiya); it was instituted in February 1990 and is made up of a number of doctors and psychologists headed by Dr Nikolai Oleinikov. Gay men and lesbians can obtain anonymous medical and psychological help from it, especially in social and personal crisis situations; they can meet qualified personnel to discuss their problems. An American postgraduate sociologist, Daniel Shluter, conducting research in Moscow, rendered particular methodological assistance to the group in the initial stages. As many as 80 people were meeting each Monday in 1991 and 1992 and the group was planning to conduct a number of research projects and to work with adolescents, including through confidential telephone calls. Unless this venture has to close through lack of funds or for ideological reasons (as a 'homosexual breeding-ground'), it could well become the embryo of the first gay culture centre in the country.

The International Symposium on Human Rights and the Fight Against AIDS, organised by the *Tema* international organisation in Moscow and Leningrad simultaneously in July 1991, marked an important political milestone in the defence of sexual minorities. The main meetings were held in large conference halls, and the country's first ever programme of gay and lesbian films was openly shown. Besides sessions devoted mainly to political issues, the organisers put on several special symposiums at which participants discussed specific questions affecting the lives of sexual minorities, their psychological wellbeing and culture, AIDS prevention and so on. The Western side was represented by radical US and Canadian gay movement leaders, lawyers, journalists and AIDS experts. The ex-Soviet side was less competently represented in so far as leading specialists were invited literally on the eve of the opening and were unable to take part, especially as they were not informed of the programme. Similarly, gay organisation leaders who did not support Roman Kalinin had been invited only at the very last moment. That turned the Symposium into more of a monologue than a discussion.

All the same, many constructive ideas were voiced; they may well help gay men and lesbians in the country better to organise their lives and struggle. What is even more important is the very fact of such a conference being held openly in the country's two largest cities, with the permission and even the assistance of the local authorities. Sensibly, the participants decided at the last moment not to parade in Red Square, confining themselves to a more modest rally accompanied by the handing out of free condoms. The Symposium was shown in a positive, if sceptical, light by the democratic media.

After the collapse of the attempted coup in August 1991, the social position of gay men and lesbians took a turn for the better. Following a long struggle and the personal intervention of the then Russian Vice-President, Sergei Shakhrai, and the St Petersburg Justice Department, the civil rights organisation Krylya ('Wings' – formerly known as 'Neva Shores') was officially registered in 1991; the organisers originally wanted to call their association 'Neva Prospect' ('Nevskaya perspektiva'), but the authorities saw that as an 'incitement to homosexualise the Neva District', so the organisers borrowed the title of Mikhail Kuzmin's famous story. This was the first official registration of gay men and lesbians in Russia.

In November 1991 Moscow City Council registered the ARGO-RISK association, which was intending to set up 'gay businesses' in Russia and publish the journal *RISK* (its first issue came out in March 1992 with a print run of 5,000). With the backing of the Medicine and Reproduction health-diagnostic centre and the *RISK* journal, the Raduga ('Rainbow') Fund was set up, embracing gay men and lesbians and their relatives, as well as doctors, journalists and persons in the field of culture. The Fund's main task is to organise a friendship service, psychological consultation and various cultural activities. The major hindrance to its activity is lack of money.

The radical tendency headed by Roman Kalinin and Yevgeniya Debrenskaya, involved in the Libertarian Party and responsible for the *Tema* paper, formed the autonomous alliance 'Liberation' in February 1992, with some 70 members. Its programme is roughly the same as that of 'Wings', but with its main reliance on politics. Its charter says that it is to hold protest meetings, to picket, demonstrate, take part in the work of state and government agencies, and even to include the security services within its structure.

Organisational confusion and ideological differences clearly hamper the work of these young organisations, but that can hardly be helped at the present stage.

Their international ties are also strengthening. In September 1991 Moscow was the venue for a round table on 'Human Rights for Gays and Lesbians in Eastern Europe'; this was within the framework of the Conference on Measuring Implementation of the Conference Resolutions on Security and Cooperation in Europe. Further, in the summer of 1992, an international conference took place in Moscow on gay and lesbian lifestyles. Information on the lives of Russian gay men and lesbians is now regularly appearing in the Western gay press.

'Blue' art was developing alongside the political movement. Anyone engaging in such activities in Brezhnev's time would certainly have found themselves behind bars – such was the tragic fate of the artist Yevgeny Kharitonov and the poet Gennady Trifonov. Today, Moscow has the highly successful homoerotic theatre of the director Roman Viktyuk. A homoerotic mood and symbolism are present in many films – though the audience is not always aware of it. The first issue of *Eros* (spring 1992) contained the short story by Stefan Zweig, *Confused Feelings*, which had been suppressed since 1927. Further, openly homoerotic poetry has begun to appear.

So the struggle is continuing.

The future of gay men and lesbians depends, in the final count, on the fate of the country as a whole. If it takes the democratic road there will evidently be decriminalisation of sexual minorities, though this will not happen without a struggle or before a new Russian criminal code is adopted. A single legislative act will hardly suffice.

If, on the other hand, reaction makes a comeback, whether fascist or communist, homosexuals will once again be driven deep underground. Even given a favourable outcome, the process is bound to be protracted, problematical and vastly different in the various regions and former republics. The country's history is not being made in California or even in Moscow, but in Russia generally, in Tatarstan, Uzbekistan, Georgia and elsewhere. That must be taken into account.

As is the case with any other social minority that cannot detach itself and form a separate independent state, the emancipation of gay men and lesbians and their social and cultural integration are two sides of the same process. They are faced, in our view, with three basic tasks.

The first is to decriminalise homosexuality as part of the overall process of democratising the country. No people can be free if it oppresses its own social minorities – and gay men and lesbians are the most numerous minority, even if they are the least visible. Decriminalisation can only be attained by the concerted effort of all democratic forces. No 'political happening' can help in this instance; that may well be effective among well-fed, happy and benevolent people, but in our situation it is likely merely to intensify general irritation and tension.

Second, the general public needs to be systematically educated. Homophobia is the result of more than reactionary policy. A public for which all sex customarily appears shameful and sordid, and which experiences a sense of alarm even over heterosexuality, is bound to regard homosexuality, about which it has heard nothing but monstrosities, with the utmost intolerance. After all, the first more or less serious discussion of homosexuality occurred only in 1988. Is there any wonder that it causes aggravation and hatred among many people? The mass media, science and the arts have a decisive role to play here.

Thirdly, a gay and lesbian subculture must be established. Homosexuals must turn their ghetto into a normal community of gay men and lesbians with its own publications, clubs, consultation and advice bureaux and suchlike, much as has happened in the West.

All these objectives are interconnected and have to be implemented simultaneously and in parallel, without shelving any of them or leaving them to someone else. This can only be done through cooperation and dialogue.

References

1. Sergei Solovyov, *Istoriya Rossii.* 3 izd (St Petersburg: 1910), p. 710.
2. See Eve Levin, *Sex and Society in the World of the Orthodox Slavs, 900–1700* (Ithaca and London: 1989), pp. 197–204. See also Simon Karlinsky, 'Russia's Gay Literature and History (11th–20th Centuries)', *Gay Sunshine*, nos 29–30 (Summer/Fall 1976).
3. For more details, see Simon Karlinsky, 'Russia's Gay Literature and Culture: the Impact of the October Revolution', in M.B. Duberman, M.M. Vicinus and G. Chauncey Jr (eds), *Hidden from History. Reclaiming the Gay and Lesbian Past* (New York: 1989).
4. Until recently, Soviet people had absolutely no knowledge of the history of Russian homosexuality; its elements appeared most frequently in the form of myths. The celebrated Russian writer Yuri Nagibin, for example, resurrected the legend of Tchaikovsky's suicide by order of a court of honour made up of former students. See Yuri Nagibin, 'Tchaikovsky: final tragedii', *Megapolis-express* 1990, no. 16, p. 13. This legend has been carefully examined by experts and rejected as utterly unproven. See Simon Karlinsky, 'Russia's Gay Literature and History'; Nina Berberova, 'Préface a l'édition de 1987' to her book *Tchaikovski* (Paris: 1987); Alexander Poznansky 'Tchaikovsky's Suicide: Myth and Reality', *19th Century Music*, vol. 11, no. 3, Spring 1988; and Alexander Poznansky, *Tchaikovsky. The Quest for the Inner Man* (New York: 1991).
5. See V.V. Rozanov, *Lyudi lunnovo sveta*, 2nd edn (St Petersburg: 1913); Vladimir Nabokov, 'Homosexualität im Russischen Strafgesetzbuch', in *Jahrbuch für sexuelle Zwischenstufen*, Band 5 (Leipzig: 1903). On Russian homosexual subculture at the turn of the century, see, besides the numerous articles of Simon Karlinsky, John E. Malmstad, *Mikhail Kuzmin: A Chronicle of His Life and Times* (London: 1978); Mikhail Kuzmin, *Sobranie stikhov*, and commentary by John E. Malmstad and Vladimir Markov (Munich: 1977), vol. 3, pp. 7–319.
6. *Marx-Engels Werke*, Band 32, p. 324: quoted in Hartmut Schultze, 'Links und linksgestrickt', *Konkret Sexualität* (1979), pp. 68–70.
7. Mark Sereisky, 'Gomosexualizm', *Bolshaya Sovetskaya Entsiklopediya*, vol. 17, pp. 593–4 (Moscow: 1930).
8. The etymology of the word is far from clear. It is often connected with either the Russian term of endearment *golubchik* ('little dove') or the concept of 'blue' noble blood, thereby hinting at exclusivity. See, for example, Wayne R. Dynes, 'Color Symbolism', in Wayne R. Dynes (ed.), *Encyclopedia of Homosexuality* (New York and London: 1990), vol. 1, p. 249. It is interesting that Dynes finds no 'blue' symbols in other countries, although the notion of 'blue love' (and 'blue movies') does exist in several other languages, including the French. See Cécile Beurdeley, *'L'Amour Bleu. Die homosexuelle Liebe in Kunst und Literatur des Abendlandes* (Cologne: 1977). It may even be connected

with the colour of moonlight: hence the poet Rozanov's reference to 'sodomites' as people of the colour of moonlight.

9. See Karlinsky's works indicated in notes 2–4 above for a more detailed bibliography.
10. A.M. Gorky, 'Predislovie – S. Schweig', in *Smutenie chuvstv. Iz zapisok starovo cheloveka* (Leningrad: 1927).
11. A.M. Gorky, *Sobranie sochineniy v 30 tomakh*, vol. 27 (Moscow: 1953), p. 238.
12. The report on Krylenko's speech was published in Sovetskaya yustitsiya, 1936, no. 7. Detailed information on Soviet homosexuals in Stalin's and post-Stalin times is available in the works of Karlinsky mentioned above. See also Joachim S. Hohmann, 'Zur rechtlichen und sozialen Problem der Homosexualität, in *Sexualforschung und politik in der Sowjetunion seit 1917* (Frankfurt am Main, Berne, New York, Paris: 1990); Siegfried Tornow, 'Ruckschritt gleich Fortschritt. Geschichte der Schwulen in Sowjet-Russland', *Siegesssaule*, 1987, no. 6.
13. See Alla Bossart, 'Sergei – I shchsif: apokrify', *Ogonyok*, 1991, no. 316, p. 15.
14. Igor Kon, 'Ponyatie druzhby v Drevnei Gretsii', *Vestnik drevnei istorii*, 1974, no. 3.
15. See, for example, Igor Kon, *Druzhba: etiko-psikhologichesky ocherk* (Moscow: 1980, 1987, 1989). It was easier to do so in foreign publications even though they also had to go through the Soviet censor. See I.S. Kon, 'Adolescent Friendship: Some Unanswered Questions for Future Research', in Steve Duck and Robin Gilmour (eds), *Personal Relationships. 2. Developing Personal Relationships* (Robin Gilmour, Academic Press, 1981), pp. 187–204.
16. See, for example, G.S. Vasilchenko (ed.), *Obshchaya sexopatologiya* (Moscow: 1977); G.S. Vasilchenko (ed.), *Chastnaya sexopatologiya* (Moscow: 1984); A.M. Svyadoshch, *Zhenskaya sexopatologiya*. 3 izd (Moscow: 1988).
17. 'Sexopatologiya', in G.S. Vasilchenko (ed.), *Spravochnik* (Moscow: 1990), pp. 429–36. We ought to stress that Professor Vasilchenko is a most educated and liberal Soviet sexopathologist of the older generation, who has always supported the idea of decriminalising homosexuality, in contrast to the majority of Soviet psychiatrists.
18. Ibid., p. 432.
19. Igor Kon, 'Psikhologiya podrostkovoi i yunosheskoi gomosexualnosti', in the collection *Diagnostika, lechenie i profilaktika polovykh rasstroistv* (Moscow: 1978).
20. A.G. Khripkova, D.V. Kolesov, *Malchik-podrostok-yunosha* (Moscow: 1982), pp. 96–100.
21. N.P. Burgasov, 'SPID v SSSR', *Literaturnaya gazeta* 7 May 1986.
22. A. Potapov, *Literaturnaya gazeta*, 20 August 1986, p. 11.

23. Alla Alova, 'Zhizn pri SPIDe', *Ogonyok*, 1988, no. 28, pp. 12–15.
24. D.N. Isayev, V.Y. Kagan, I.S. Kon, 'Formirovanie sexualnoi orient-atsii', in D.N. Isayev, V.Y. Kagan, *Psikhogigiena pola u detei. Rukovodstvo dlya vrachei* (Leningrad: 1986), pp. 47–65.
25. I.S. Kon, *Vvedenie v sexologiyu* (Moscow: 1988; 2nd edn 1989; transl. into Ukrainian, Kiev 1991; abridged Estonian edn, Tallinn 1987).
26. Igor Kon, *Psikhologiya rannei yunosti. Kniga dlya uchitelya* (Moscow: 1989), pp. 223–8.
27. See M. Shargorodsky and P. Osipov, *Kurs sovetskovo ugolovncwo prava*, vol. 3 (Leningrad: 1973).
28. See, for example, the polemic in the weekly *Argumenty i fakty*, 1990, no. 12: the item by V. Kachanov and the Kon article 'Zakon i polovye prestupleniya'.
29. Statistics are here reproduced with permission from the All-Union Public Opinion Centre.
30. Vladislav Likhotlitov, 'Obnazhonnaya natura – sevodnya i yezhednevno. Interview s Valentinom Pokrovskim', *Megapolis-express*, 7 February 1991, no. 6, p. 14.
31. All the figures cited here are taken from K.K. Borisenko, *Zabolevaniya, peredavayemye polvym putyom, u muzhchin-gomosexualistov (diagnostika, taktika vedeniya, lechenie) Metodicheskie rekomendatsii* (Moscow: 1990).
32. See Lev Samoilov (pseudonym), 'Etnografia lagerya', *Sovetskaya etnografia*, 1990, no. 1; see also V. Kozlovsky, 'Argo russkoi gomosexualnoi subkultury'.
33. Alexander Eckstein, 'Dnevnik stukacha', *Ogonyok*, 1990, no. 35, p. 29.
34. See, for example, Robert N. Boyd, *Sex Behind Bars* (San Francisco: 1984).
35. See, for example, Galina Toktalieva, 'Olya & Yulia', *Sobesednik*, November 1989, no. 46, p. 11.
36. See *Sexopatologiya. Spravochnik* (Moscow: 1991).
37. *SPID-info*, 1990, no. 5, p. 5.
38. See *Ogonyok*, 1991, no. 12, p. 23.
39. Incidentally, 'Red Square' is not a communist symbol but an ancient Russian name – 'red' being the same word as 'beautiful' in Old Russian.
40. 'Sex-menshinstva i Mossovet: lyubov i soglasie', *Semya*, 1990, no. 47, p. 2.
41. V. Andreyev, 'Vozvrashchayas k *Teme*', *Pravda*, 5 May 1991, p. 3.
42. Igor Kon, 'Levshu ne pereuchish', *Argumenty i fakty*, 1990, no. 51, p. 8.
43. S. Mitrofanov, 'Libertariantsy: prezident mozhet byt gomosexualistom', *Kommersant*, 29 April–6 May 1991, no. 18, p. 10.
44. *Literaturnaya gazeta*, 22 May 1991, p. 2.

5

Soviet Beauty Contests

ELIZABETH WATERS

Meditsinskaya gazeta, covering the third Moscow Beauty Contest in 1991, suggested that society had yet to decide what it wanted a beauty queen to be: recipient of poetic odes, coat-hanger for the latest fashions, or sex symbol; should she be a Tatiana Larina (the principled and inaccessible heroine of Pushkin's *Yevgeny Onegin*), a top model for a house of fashion, or a Russian Marilyn Monroe?[1] Since 1988, when the first contests were held in the USSR, beauty queens have certainly fulfilled all three of these roles, and it is precisely this combination of functions that gave them a highly visible and symbolic place under perestroika.

Although by the 1980s the beauty contest had established itself firmly in both Poland and Yugoslavia, it was still unknown in the USSR, where ideologists considered such public displays of the female body as typically bourgeois behaviour, decadent and depraved, 'alien to the socialist way of life'. Reality was rather more complex. In the 1970s and early 1980s, detente and the country's rising profile as a trading partner and tourist destination for the industrialising nations was bringing greater access to Western culture and style, and the major European cities in particular, and the young in particular came under their influences. Imported Marlboro cigarettes and Christian Dior perfumes were sought-after *defitsitnye* items; denim jeans and pop records by the latest groups sold on the black market for exorbitant prices. By the same routes, legal and illegal, images of Western women infiltrated and made their mark on the national consciousness. Young Soviet women wore bikinis on the beach and raised hemlines in city streets; Soviet advertising and cinema began to incorporate in their repertoire 'tasteful' female nudity. Wide sections of the Soviet public, in other words, were growing accustomed to the female body on public display, to the female body as a recognised source of visual pleasure.

Perestroika and the Example of the West

Perestroika, as one might expect, encouraged a reappraisal of the official view on beauty contests and – the ground already having been so well prepared – found in their favour. At the end of Mikhail Gorbachov's third year in office, photographs and reports of beauty queens began to appear in the press. In March 1988, over 100 contestants paraded in ballgowns and swimsuits before a jury in Vilnius, the capital of Lithuania;[2] a few weeks later a similar scene took place in Riga, the capital of the neighbouring republic of Latvia.[3] Leningrad, Odessa, Kiev and other cities soon followed suit. Beauty contests were staged even in the Muslim republics of Central Asia, where in the 1920s women had been murdered for abandoning their veils. One such, held in July 1988 in Tashkent, Uzbekistan, advertised itself as a native show rather than a beauty contest, though, as *Pravda vostoka* pointed out, Western conventions were in fact observed closely, even to the point of a swimsuit parade; the event apparently attracted more spectators and photo-correspondents than the stadium in which it was held 'had ever seen before'.[4] The local paper in Baku, capital of another Muslim republic, Azerbaidzhan, gave a positive write-up to a beauty pageant organised in one of the city squares, also in July, and certainly the photograph which accompanied the article showed a large and satisfied crowd. In November, at the Khimvolkno Palace of Culture and Technology, the provincial Belorussian town of Belta chose its Miss Festival, a local banking employee.[5] A few weeks later Moscow staged an ambitiously large-scale Miss Charm contest, and in May 1989, amid considerable national and international publicity, the capital was host to an 'All-Union Beauty Contest', which culminated in the selection of the first Miss USSR.

Reporting the Vilnius contest in March 1988, an *Izvestiya* correspondent remarked: 'There's only one thing I don't understand – and that's why this contest was the first.'[6] The climate of opinion in the USSR was changing so fast and fundamentally that it was already hard to fathom why beauty pageants should have ever been found unacceptable. The official rejection of cold war mentalities was opening the gates to criticisms of domestic shortcomings and to discussion of Western lifestyles in other thån negative tones. In this context, to stage beauty contests was confirmation of the break with the 'stagnant' past, proof that the Soviet Union had set its face towards the 'civilised' world. The political statement encoded in the beauty contest was part of its appeal to the reform-minded. Despite the propaganda of the late 1970s and early 1980s which lauded the Soviet Union's 'mature socialism' and the good life it purported to sustain, an increasingly sophisticated urban public, convinced of the emptiness of Soviet ideology and conversant with the standards of living available in industrialised countries outside the Eastern Bloc, looked to the West for its model in ever larger numbers. The West was seen as exemplar not only of political democracy but also of lifestyle; indeed, before Gorbachov came to power, the consumer goods and modes of leisure of the 'capitalist countries' were the object of far more interest than their parliamentary systems. It was perestroika that added the political dimension and encouraged the view that Western lifestyles and democratic values were interconnected, indeed mutually interdependent. The beauty contest could thus be seen as doubly justified, both a political and cultural prerequisite. This is not to suggest that the arrival of the Soviet beauty queen was greeted with a sophisticated commentary on her cause and significance. But the unspoken assumption of her progressive credentials helps explain how pageants could take their place so quickly as a 'natural' part of life, why they were given prominent and uncritical space in pro-reform publications like *Moscow News*, and what it was that motivated the well-known political commentator Vladimir Pozner to volunteer to contact beauty contest organisers while on a trip to the United States, and the star of the Bolshoi Ballet, Yekaterina Maximova, to agree to serve as Patron of the All-Union Beauty Contest.[7]

Apart from signifying the break with old ideologies, beauty contests offered practical opportunities, albeit on a small scale, for integration into the new world order. Experts from the Miss Poland contest bureau were called in to direct the Miss Charm pageant in Moscow in 1989;[8] the Lithuanians also established links with their Polish neighbours and invited Miss Polonia 1988 to attend their competition;[9] the Miss Charm contest in Moscow was billed to include contestants from Scandinavia, West Germany, Singapore and well over 20 other foreign countries.[10] Before long the traffic in beauty contestants was moving in both directions. Although some Soviet beauty queens apparently experienced difficulties obtaining permission from the authorities to travel abroad to compete in contests, the press carried stories of passports issued and titles won. Saltanat Kamolieva from Alma-Ata was selected to participate in the Miss Asia 88 competition in London and came second; Yekaterina Chilichkina won a European beauty contest in Helsinki.[11]

Beauty contests reflected the USSR's fresh approach to business as well as to culture and politics. It was recognised that pageants had an economic aspect which, as hostility to the market waned, could be faced dispassionately. It was Western firms that took the initiative. Aware of the potential of the large Soviet market for clothes of stylish Western cut and of the USSR's untapped supply of potential models, the German firm Burda Moden, partner in a joint venture to produce a fashion magazine in Russian, became a promoter of beauty contests. Two Americans, Eileen and Gerry Ford, in Moscow on fashion business, saw a beauty pageant on television and decided the time was ripe to invite the USSR to take part in their international Supermodel contest in Los Angeles.

The economic role of beauty contests has received greater coverage in the Russian and Commonwealth press than it does in day-to-day reporting in the West. In October 1988 the magazine *Sputnik* used a discussion of pageants to lament the underdeveloped state of the fashion industry. *Izvestiya* noted that the clothing industry 'occupied second place in the world in terms of volume of production' and explained how beauty contests were an essential part of its functioning: successful participants gained publicity and made themselves a reputation; the fashion industry was introduced to potential models.[12] This is certainly an angle that feature articles in the Western quality press occasionally take, but not something to which the popular press often alludes.

Soviet beauty contests from the very beginning attracted the attention of the country's new entrepreneurs: Tonis participated in the organisation of Miss Riga 1988;[13] the Dnepropetrovsk Centre of Scientific and Technical Creativity, ('Impulse') was one of the sponsors of Miss Charm 1989. Private ventures of this type had only recently been legalised and were initially hobbled by restrictions on their rights to conduct business and hire labour; they were few and far between, small-scale and low-budget, and more often than not obstructed by local communist elites. In other words, if beauty contests were to be organised in a big way it was inevitable that the official apparatus would, at least initially, be the prime mover.

Although perestroika was successfully challenging the hegemony the Party had exercised for decades over every aspect of Soviet life, it could not produce alternatives overnight, could not in this case produce at a stroke someone like the British beauty contest entrepreneur Eric Morley. Hence the strange spectacle, to the Western eye, of communists, particularly the Young Communist League (Komsomol), acting as major promoters of beauty contests. It was the Central Committee of the Tadzhik Komsomol that in the autumn of 1988 phoned the Komsomol secretary of the Dushanbe Medical Institute and instructed him to select a handful of pretty students for the Miss Asia competition. The secretary, accordingly, went to the Institute's crowded main entrance hall and persuaded eight likely looking candidates to take part in an impromptu contest for the title of Miss Tadzhikistan 88, with himself and representatives of the Ministry of Culture and the Komsomol as judges.[14]

Similarly, Tashkent Beauty 88 was held in the city's House of Youth under the auspices of the Central Committee of the Lenin Komsomol of Uzbekistan; Miss Riga-88 was sponsored by the city's Komsomol Committee and Youth Centre; and Saltanat Kamoliev's trip to London to take part in the Miss Asia competition was financed by the Fund for Social Inventions of the national young communist newspaper *Komsomolskaya pravda*. Beauty contests were wholeheartedly accepted as profit-making events, but Western business practices were modified to meet the prevailing Soviet conditions.

When pageant organiser G. Danishevsky was asked whether the Moscow beauty Contest, of which he was artistic director, would be modelled on Western pageants like Miss World and Miss Universe, he replied: 'Why reinvent the bicycle?'[15] An examination of the format of Soviet beauty contests indicates that, regardless of the nature of their financial backing, they have indeed for the most part accepted the regulations current in the West.

Major Soviet beauty contests have adopted the standard Western practice of requiring contestants to be unmarried and childless. The press has explained these rulings without protest. One journalist remarked philosophically, 'Such are the international regulations. Well, beauty demands sacrifice.'[16] Another correspondent poked fun at a reader who argued that despite having children and doing housework, married women could win beauty contests; no comment, he said playfully, he wanted to keep on the right side of his readers.[17] Soviet beauty contests have, similarly, looked for types of beauty that conform to accepted Western norms. The Vilnius competition was advertised as open to women with an attractive exterior, a good figure and the ability to hold themselves well. The 1989 Miss USSR contest invited applications from 'members of the "fair sex" from 17 to 27 who are attractive and pleasant, who have slender figures, who move and dance well, who know the rules of etiquette and have a sense of humour'.[18]

The slender figure is not something that Soviet culture has always equated with beauty. The peasantry, who until recently made up the majority of the population, continued to equate bulk with beauty long after the educated sections of society began to adopt Western stereotypes. A solidly built woman was popularly regarded as healthy, capable of childbearing and hard work, and attractive. Industrialisation and its attendant social and cultural revolutions have weakened the force of these equations and over the past two decades the slender beauty has taken firm root in urban culture. There was never any question that Soviet pageants would challenge the modern Western ideal of female physical attractiveness.

On a different note, Soviet beauty contests have also approached the Western norm in the number of scandals they generate. The financial investments made in pageants are considerable and the image of the everyday superwoman, perfect in body and conventional in lifestyle, that beauty queens are expected to personify is demanding. Drama and conflict often ensue. In recent years, one American beauty queen lost her title when she was discovered to be expecting a baby, another suffered the same fate after sexually explicit photographs of her with another woman were published.[19] In the Soviet Union the problem was less the lapses of the contestants than the country's endemic inefficiency and corruption. At the first Miss Moscow competition, in June 1988, there were angry and public recriminations when the announcer, Leonid Yakubovich, criticised the competition organisers and accused Yuri Blaginin, a local Komsomol official, of doing his best to ruin the event. In addition, there were reports that the winner of the competition had been selected before the final took place and contestants notified in advance of the decision.[20] Similar rumours circulated after a contest in Tashkent: some said the 'authorities' had picked the winner; others that the 'mafia' had bribed the organisers to crown their preferred contestant; a third story had it that the wrong contestant won because the jury made a mistake in adding up the scores.[21]

Sovietisation of the Contests

Along with these similarities to the West, the first Soviet beauty
contests displayed in their format, as in their finances, a number of
differences determined by the specificities of the local environment.
The casual Western attitude to exposing the female body to public
gaze was still held at arms' length. A beauty show held in the Central
Asian republic of Tadzhikistan dispensed with the parade of contestants in bathing costumes in deference to local Muslim sensibilities.
Elsewhere, if such parades took place media attention was not
initially drawn to them. Reports in the press on beauty contests were
often accompanied by photographs, but these were of women in
national costume and ballgowns rather than bathing costumes. The
prevailing understanding of beauty still owed much to the nineteenth-
century notion of women as beings of a superior virtue and morality,
which had survived the Revolution and persisted into the 1980s
through the exposure of generations of Soviet schoolchildren to the
classics of Russian literature. The connotations of beauty were
redemption, virtue and hope rather than pleasure and danger,
romance and eroticism. It was no coincidence that *Izvestiya* picked up
on Eileen Ford's view, expressed at a press conference, that the
fashion industry was not just about making money, that it had a
higher purpose.

The idea of the spiritual essence of beauty found a ready resonance
in Soviet thinking. One beauty queen, Yekaterina Chilichkina, was
reported as saying that the aim of the beauty contest was not only to
provide entertainment but also to impart warmth and charm to life; in
addition, in her view, contests could inspire in men those knightly
feelings towards the female sex that they had lost. Beauty pageants
helped the women who took part in them as well as the audience, it
was said. Psychologists were cited to the effect that feeling beautiful
improved woman's sense of wellbeing and her work performance.[22]
An Azerbaidzhani journalist, in an article entitled 'Every Baku
Woman is a Beauty', praised pageants for providing contestants with
the opportunity to discover their basic feminine qualities, 'charm,
grace, resourcefulness and wit'.[23] One contest, held in an
Educational-Labour Colony for underage offenders in the Russian
town of Ryazan, was even credited with a 'miracle': Irina Zhukova,
committed for two years for theft, was aggressive and truculent, the
despair of her warders, until she became a beauty queen. After her

victory in the contest she apparently 'melted', her 'cynicism and unnaturally abrasive manner' disappearing without trace.[24] The beauty contest, in short, was presented as a public-spirited institution. As *Sputnik* put it: 'We need these contests for the stimulation of public opinion, need them for the development of taste, need them for the self-confidence without which the average women can't live a truly human life.'[25] According to the jury of the Moscow beauty contest, 'We all need beauty contests.'[26]

Press coverage of the contests, especially the frequent interviews with participants and winners, helped further to 'Sovietise' them, to present them in a manner designed to win the widest public acceptance. Beauty queens came from ordinary Soviet families (we learn about their parents, their siblings); their reassuringly conventional lives and aspirations were described (we hear about their hobbies, their studies, their plans for the future). Yekaterina Chilichkina works for a cooperative advertising agency, studies ballroom dancing, wants to become a teacher but has not yet managed to find herself a college place. Asked whether she likes cooking, she admits that her father is the better chef. None of the family is in good health, she confides, and her New Year's wish is for an end to their illnesses.[27] Maria Kalinina, the winner of the Moscow 1988 contest, answers queries about her brothers and sisters and her favourite writer. She says her father thought the beauty competition sounded interesting and was keen for her to enter, while her mother was a bit nervous at the idea.[28] Saltanat Kamolieva, the runner-up in the Miss Asia competition, is introduced in *Sovetskaya Belorussia* as follow: 'The beauty from Alma-Ata is 20 years old. She is a correspondence student at the Abai Kazakh Teacher Training Institute. She grew up in a large and friendly family.' Her mother, the paper elaborates, works on the railways and her father for Kazakh radio. As a result of her success many attractive offers have come her way, but 'she remains the same as before, polite and sociable'.[29] Another newspaper quotes her as saying: 'I have three sisters. And though I've been away from them for just a short time, I've missed them very much. Really I'm not a queen at all but an ordinary Alma-Ata girl who has been very lucky . . .'[30]

Indeed, so thoroughly were beauty contests 'Sovietised' that the language they use and the language used to discuss them sometimes appeared to have been plucked straight from Party political prose. Contest organisers, for example, have been said to form *orgkomitety*, while *Sovetskaya Belorussia*, reporting on a press conference in preparation for the first All-Union Beauty contest wrote:

> the secretary of the USSR Union of Cinematography, V. Tikhonov, and other speakers, noted that we are faced with much painstaking work, and it is essential that in addressing it the organisational experience of previous contests, including the Moscow ones, be taken into consideration.[31]

So far I have emphasised the ease with which beauty contests in the first twelve months of their existence fitted into the Soviet scene, explaining this with reference to the growing acceptance of the female body as public icon on the one hand, and their successful Sovietisation on the other. The beauty queen was made compatible with existing conventions of Soviet womanhood. Both popular and academic opinion in the former USSR has placed considerable emphasis on sexual difference, assigning to men the active, assertive sphere, to women the decorous one. Although most women are in employment, it is their other jobs as wives and mothers, creating the right material and psychological environment for family and social life, that are seen as their true vocation. Personal presentation, it is constantly reiterated, contributes to the success of the enterprise: women are loving, caring *and* beautiful. Provision of the opportunity for women both to participate in the workforce and at the same time fulfil the special demands of their femininity has been the hallmark of the Soviet synthesis of women's emancipation. Thus the first All-Union Beauty Contest could be scheduled without irony for 8 March, International Woman's Day. Soviet society had apparently forgotten that there existed a critical perspective on beauty contests; certainly no mention was made in the Soviet media at this time of the fact that in the West, from the late 1960s, pageants had come under fire from those protesting at the commercial exploitation of the female body. In this instance the Soviet Union was slow to follow the Western lead, and a condemnation of beauty contests, when it was eventually voiced, came initially from the conservatives rather than the radicals.

In the second half of the 1980s the rejection of Western economic, cultural and political models, previously official government policy, came to be identified with a particular political platform, conservative and (in Russia) Slavophile. Perestroika, its adherents alleged, was lifting the barriers to pernicious Western influences. While they targeted the same evils as the traditional Soviet critique, their concern was to preserve Russian (or other ethnic) rather than socialist morality and to focus on the alienation of the Russians (or other national groups) from their real roots in indigenous cultures. In the ultra-conservative journal, *Nash sovremennik*, the writer Valentin Rasputin attacked rock music, pornography and beauty contests. On the last topic he was amusing and ironical. He reported that a Russian Orthodox priest had been flown in from Paris to sit on the jury of the Moscow Miss Charm contest. He held up for ridicule the spectacle of the Young Communist League pronouncing such diversions to be 'important new forms of youth entertainment'. And he protested that it was not in the Russian tradition to expose the female body for public viewing.[32] Similar concerns were reflected in a reader's letter to *Pravda* bemoaning the low standards of the mass media, singling out rock and pop music on television for special criticism. Young people became black marketeers and prostitutes, the reader declared; country girls moved to the cities 'where there are beauty contests, cafes and video parlours with erotic films', and as a consequence their lives were ruined.[33]

Both Valentin Rasputin and the *Pravda* reader linked beauty contests and pornography, just as in the past, before perestroika, the official Soviet critique of the commercialisation of the female body had done. Such connection was made particularly resonant in 1989 and 1990 by the sudden and rapid spread of pornography. For years copies of *Playboy* had been smuggled into the Soviet Union, and more recently pornographic videos followed the same path from West to East. Border guards were vigilant, however, and the amount of material that evaded them was relatively tiny and correspondingly expensive. But in 1989 the relaxation of customs regulations and the access of cooperatives to printing equipment began dramatically to increase the circulation of pornography. Pin-ups and sex manuals were sold in the streets; the mushrooming video salons found that soft porn guaranteed an audience and a handsome profit; at the more intellectual end of the market, a number of exhibitions of erotica took place.[34] It was not only the conservative camp that responded to the proliferation of sexually explicit images of women. Their ubiquity could not but have an impact on popular perceptions of the female body and subtly change the way in which beauty contestants were regarded: an element of ambiguity was introduced into the meaning of the beauty queen; her innocence and wholesomeness were thrown open to dispute.

The Search for Miss USSR

The first All-Union Beauty Contest, held in the spring of 1989, illustrates well the combination of Western and native ingredients that went into the making of the Soviet pageant. It also demonstrates the instability of the mixture – the intrusion of sensuality and the growing dominance of Western business and cultural formulae.[35]

When the All-Union Beauty Contest was initially mentioned in the press, a good twelve months before Miss USSR was finally crowned in May 1989 (it proved impossible to meet the 8 March deadline), an impressive rollcall of organisations was said to be involved in the project: USSR Goskino; the Union of Cinematographers; TASS and Mosfilm; American, West German and French firms. The All-Union Directory on the Organisation of Mass Spectacles was also listed. *Sovetskaya Belorussia* revealed that the Directory was in fact one of the new private economic ventures, named Venets ('Crown'). Other media reports, probably responding to residual uncertainties about private enterprise, omitted this fact, leaving readers possibly to assume that with such an imposing title the Directory was an official body. Later accounts in the press, when the market had become more acceptable, left no room for doubt about the Directory's status, referring to it simply as Crown. By the time a BBC camera team arrived to make its documentary, 'Inside Story – Miss USSR', the official sponsors had faded into the background. Their role was largely supportive (though in the event, as we shall see, this proved to be of the utmost importance) and ceremonial (the Director of Mosfilm would address a press conference, and a People's Artist would have her photo taken on stage with finalists). Crown took responsibility, more or less single-handedly, for organising the event.

Far from marking the triumph of native entrepreneurial capitalism, this situation reflected the difficulties faced by the embryonic Soviet market. Many Western firms, initially eager to make money in the Soviet Union, found that profits eluded them because of obstructions placed in their path by the Soviet authorities and sometimes because their products were hard to sell at commercial prices, given the worthlessness of the rouble and the limited income of most Soviet citizens. The sponsors who came forward to fund Soviet projects had to be willing to take a risk and often, by the same token, were themselves a risk: they did not always play according to the rules and were sometimes unreliable and failed to fulfil obligations – as Crown discovered. At first it had negotiated with an English firm, but soon came under the spell of the Afro-Arab Industrial Shipping Company, whose representative, a Dr Monsor, made glittering promises of foreign investment and of foreign costumes and cosmetics for the contestants. Right up until the eve of the contest he continued to insist that the arrival of his goods was imminent, only at the eleventh hour admitting that nothing was arranged and saying that he no longer wanted to be associated with the Miss USSR contest. It was at this point that the system of sponsorship and Crown's informal ties with the theatre world paid off. Music and lighting, costumes and cosmetics were begged and borrowed, loaned and donated. The show went on.

Disputes with the Afro-Arab Shipping Company were not the only problems with which Crown had to contend. The Lithuanian authorities made the competition an occasion to assert their sovereignty and refused to allow their queen to take part in an 'All-Union' contest. In a show of entrepreneurial solidarity, Crown had agreed not to hold a first round in the capital, so as not to compete with the Moscow beauty contest scheduled for later that year, but in consequence until the last minute was without Moscow finalists.[36] While financial and organisational difficulties stemmed from specific Soviet conditions – the fragility of the market, the novelty of the enterprise – there were other problems with a specifically modern, Western edge: Inga Levinson, winner of a first-round contest in Odessa and a Crown calendar girl, was discovered to be married and a mother; while no sooner had Iulia Sukhanova been crowned Miss USSR than she questioned the legality of contracts she had signed, which gave Crown control over her future career and earnings. Inga Levinson was disqualified. Iulia Sukhanova was threatened with the loss of her title, and though the matter was eventually settled there was, according to an American newspaper, further ill-feeling when Crown's director, Yuri Kushnerov, threatened to prevent her from visiting the United States unless he accompanied her 'alone'; she, undeterred, complained to the press 'and the director was forced to stand down'.[37]

The organisers had never been under any illusions that their project was an easy one. 'What we're trying to do is new and we're not quite up to it yet,' one of them admitted. They worked extremely hard to raise themselves and the contestants to world standards. The 35 finalists were brought to Moscow for three weeks of intensive training. The pedagogical tone adopted by Crown was thoroughly Soviet – girls who turned up late for sessions were reminded that this was no way to treat a 'teacher' or a 'comrade', that respect for the 'collective' was a vital necessity – but the training was thoroughly Western: the contestants spent hours in the gym getting into shape, and more time with hairdressers and beauticians. They also, more unusually, were provided with lectures on aesthetics and later, at the rehearsals, with a choreographer to teach them how to move gracefully across a stage. These lessons were deemed important by the organisers, who believed that Soviet women, unless schooled to do otherwise, moved in a sexually suggestive way. The respectability of the beauty contest could no longer be taken for granted as it had been in the days before the rise of pornography. Aware that the major foreign beauty contests rejected the 'vulgar', the organisers wanted to prevent a display of instinctive Soviet sensuality. But despite their efforts to distance themselves from 'vulgarity', they did include in their programme of entertainment at least one cabaret item in questionable taste and distributed swimsuits to contestants that were far more revealing than considered appropriate by Western pageants. No doubt the organisers were themselves unclear precisely where the West drew the line in matters of vulgarity and, moreover, as businesspeople, they perhaps could not resist taking advantage of the relaxation in censorship and the consumer demand for sexual titillation.

For the most part, however, as the All-Union Beauty Contest evolved from draft plan to final product, it approximated increasingly to the Western model. During the first round of contests, held across the country in the major cities, the organisers had allowed certain concessions to local customs. Girls competing in Dushanbe, the capital of Muslim Tadzhikistan, were spared a swimsuit parade and instead invited to dance in 'sportive' costume (though, oddly, this contest featured male bodybuilders as a cabaret item). The jury chose a Tadzhik girl of traditional dress and modest demeanour as beauty queen, or rather as Princess of the Tadzhik New Year, the title being another concession to local custom. But it was the runners-up, two modern misses, one Russian and the other Tadzhik, who went forward to the final round in Moscow.

Initially contestants were to do more than simply put themselves on display: they were to take the initiative in deciding how the contest would be run, they would dance, mime, recite, perhaps play chess.[38]

'[T]heir aesthetic tastes, their erudition, their sense of humour, ability to adapt in various situations' would also, it was promised, be taken into consideration.[39] As late as the eve of the competition, contestants entered for Miss Cinema (competitions for top actress and top model were also part of the programme) were working on dramatic sketches to be performed as part of the competition: one saw herself as Scheherazade, another as Snow White. But just as the early plans to assess mime and chess, learning and laughter came to nothing, the sketches too were scrapped in favour of the more conventional interviews with the compere. So apart from an ethnic touch to the opening of the final contest, when contestants picked their numbers from 35 matryoshka dolls, the proceedings followed the Western pattern. Contestants met representatives of the press on a river boat ride; they were driven to the contest venue in horse-drawn carriages; a navy band was on hand to sound a welcome; no photo-opportunity was left unutilised. The show itself consisted of the conventional parades in national costumes, ballgowns and swim-suits, interspersed with song and dance provided by professional entertainers.

The All-Union Beauty Contest was judged to have fulfilled its promise. According to the BBC, it was an 'almost seamless spectacle of Soviet pulchritude'. *Vechernaya Moskva* considered the contest had 'undoubtedly been a success'.[40] A second Miss USSR competition followed in 1990, by which time Crown had apparently consolidated its financial position and established itself as the premier contest-organising body. On this occasion contestants were obliged to sign an even stricter set of terms: to agree not only that if they became Miss USSR all contracts would be negotiated through Crown (which was entitled to a percentage of their earnings) but that, furthermore, if they were for any reason stripped of their title they would make no public statements on the matter, a stipulation that moved *Pravda* to call them 'serf queens'[41] though not, significantly, to reject the principle of the participation of private enterprise in the organisation of beauty pageants. The market had received recognition, and although official organisations did not retire from the business entirely, they took a lower profile. Burda Moden retained its interest in the Moscow beauty contest – it was co-sponsor with *Moskovsky komsomolets* – and the Soviet fashion industry began to take an interest, the noted designer Vyacheslav Zaitsev producing costumes for the contestants.[42]

A More Critical Perspective

The association between pageants and political reform did not vanish. At the beginning of 1991 the Russian-language pro-independence *Baltiyskoe vremya* ran a front-page article on Iulia Naumenko, Miss Photo Baltica 90. 'The day after the competition', it informed its readers, 'she went to church to commune with God, who is the complete embodiment of beauty.' The contest had taken place in December 1990, a time of tension in relations between the Baltic parliaments and the Kremlin, and the correspondent asked Miss Baltica to comment on the political situation. People are calm, confident and united, she said. 'One senses,' she continued, 'that they are really moving towards liberation.'[43] The beauty queen here emerges as Guardian of Spiritual Values – a role that reformers as much as conservatives have laid claim to – and Prophet of Nationhood. A report on the Miss Baltic Sea contest in Leningrad early in 1991 was used by another journalist to make an environmental point:

> Unfortunately the shores of the Baltic on which the charming feet of the contestants walk is covered with patches of oil. The sea is sick. It would be a good thing if the future success of these girls could, at least a little, improve its health.[44]

Just how the success of 'these girls' was capable of helping the environment remains unexplained, but again beauty contestants were clearly identified with a progressive cause.

By this time, however, Soviet beauty contests were being subjected to the radical critique with which we are familiar in the West. Svetlana Kusnitsina, a Soviet journalist interviewed by the BBC 'Inside Story' team, thought it 'strange that Soviet people should take the most vulgar aspects of Western life and look upon them as models of a liberal society'.[45] Subsequent comment has been more directly condemnatory and has often linked beauty contests with pornography. *Novoe vremya*, in the autumn of 1990, published an article by a German writer on sexual problems which advocated government measures to halt the spread of pornography and was highly critical of beauty contests. 'Whatever is said on this subject', he wrote, 'there can be no doubt that [the contests] treat women as a sexual object.'[46] The philosopher and feminist, Olga Voronina, labelled beauty contests little more than 'porno shows'.[47] Russian and Commonwealth feminists are, however, divided in their views on the commercial exploitation of the female body. Anastasia Posadskaya and Valentina Konstantinova, two members of the Moscow Centre for Gender Studies, have argued that censorship is a greater evil than exploitation of women's bodies and therefore oppose a campaign against pornography.[48]

'Inside Story' took another approach, emphasising the way women saw pageants as a means to an end. Few women of course make it to the top and those that do often find, as Maria Kalinina did, that victory is less sweet in reality than expectation. She discovered that her prize, a year-long modelling contract with a West Germany agency, was not the golden opportunity she had been led to believe: 'I asked if I needed high heels, and they said I needed to type, as I'd be doing office work.'[49] But never the less, just as contest organisers needed contestants in their attempt to make profit, so contestants needed contests in their attempt to make something of their lives. The beauty pageant was an opportunity to seek escape from an existence that, 'statistically, is likely to be grim'; it opened up the possibility of a future that might be finer, more comfortable, more beautiful. Contestants were concerned not about women *en masse* – about whether the contest was a good or a bad thing for the female sex in general – but about themselves in particular, about the benefits that might be in it for them as individuals. Miss Vilnius, in her interview with the BBC, said she wanted to change her life and that beauty contests would give her the opportunity to travel. One of the Tadzhik finalists in the All-Union Beauty Contest believed her participation offered a chance to find interesting work and to meet interesting people. Miss Volgograd agreed that it was 'a way out'; it was 'a breath of fresh air', her boyfriend added.

The spread of explicitly sexual images of women has undoubtedly intruded sensuality into the beauty contests and introduced ambiguity into their meaning. At the same time, the increasing currency of women's bodies as commodities has encouraged specialisation and differentiation in the significance attached to their representation. The Russian (and other nationalities') beauty contest is adopting the status it occupies in the West, at the respectable end of the range of spectacles of the female body. Beauty contests are likely in the future to draw their popularity partly from the pleasures of the forbidden that they still tenuously carry, but it is largely their very accessibility and respectability that will guarantee audiences.

Beauty contests continue to be staged in the former USSR in large numbers in a variety of venues, from kindergartens[50] to the KGB.[51]

Their role is bound to change, however, as the shoots of the new take root. As perestroika develops, as the transition to modernity proceeds, the beauty contest will inevitably be relegated to the margins. Its current visibility has been the product of a particular combination of factors: the long-frustrated desire for Western style, the sudden emergence of the market, and the freedom granted by glasnost to break old taboos, to explore femininity and sensuality. The spiritual, economic and sexual functions of the beauty contest to which *Meditsinskaya gazeta* alluded – and to which I have added the political function – will be performed in the future by a range of social institutions, by a diversifying cultural life, by the fashion and sex industries, and by an expanding civil society.

For a moment, however, the beauty contest came to be a symbol of the new dispensation, a measure of the distance the country had travelled since the days of 'stagnation'. At the beginning of 1991 *Sovetskaya kultura* published four photographs under the title 'Signs of the Times'. One was of Soviet tanks leaving Eastern Europe, another of soldiers guarding a statue of Lenin from protesters, a third was of Garri Kasparov, chess champion turned radical politician; its fourth visual image of perestroika was of a beauty contest line-up.[52] Beauty contests encapsulated people's hopes for democracy and prosperity. To a country threatened by ethnic unrest and economic uncertainty, they appeared to offer a vision of consensus: might not young women, wholesome and attractive, help to heal divisions? Might they not prove that 'beauty can save the world'?

Acknowledgements

I would like to thank Andrei Bondarev, Garrick Dombrovski and Alexander Trapeznik for their research assistance. I would also like to thank the Australian National University–Moscow State University Exchange Programme under whose auspices I spent five months in Moscow in 1989–90 and was able to observe firsthand the beauty contest phenomenon.

References

1. A. Semyonov, 'Golaya koroleva', *Meditsinskaya gazeta*, 11 January 1991.

2. A. Chekuolis, 'Nekrasivykh v Vilniuse net', *Izvestiya*, 13 March 1988.
3. K. Markarian, 'Miss Riga-88', *Izvestiya*, 28 April 1988.
4. S. Olgin, 'Ten na korone, ili kak ne nado provodit konkursy krasoty', *Pravda vostoka*, 30 June 1988.
5. E. Bulova, 'Pobeditelnitsa konkursa', *Sovetskaya Belorussia*, 24 November 1988.
6. Chekuolis, 'Nekrasivykh v Vilniuse net'.
7. A. Mosesov, 'Kto pervaya krasavitsa stolitsa?', *Sovetskaya kultura*, 16 April 1988.
8. S. Cherepenin, 'I gryanet bal krasoty', *Sovetskaya kultura*, 1 January 1989.
9. Chekuolis, 'Nekrasivykh v Vilniuse net'.
10. Cherepenin, 'I gryanet bal krasoty'.
11. 'Miss Azia', *Sovetskaya Belorussia*, 31 December 1988; 'Miss Yevropa-88', *Izvestiya*, 15 November 1988.
12. N. Kishchik, 'Faktor "iks" v vybore krasavitsy', *Izvestiya*, 7 October 1988.
13. Makarian, 'Miss Riga-88'.
14. K. Klyutkin, 'Zamira, Miss Tadzhikistan', *Kommunist Tadzhikistana*, 30 November 1988.
15. Mosesov, 'Kto pervaya krasavitsa stolitsa?'
16. 'Kto v Soyuze vsekh milee?', *Sovetskaya Belorussia*, 1 August 1988.
17. 'Skolko let koroleve?', *Sovetskaya kultura*, 12 January 1989.
18. Mosesov, 'Kto pervaya krasavitsa stolitsa?'
19. A. Marks, 'Stripping Miss America: the Man who Dethroned Vanessa Williams Reveals All,' *Philadelphia Magazine*, September 1989.
20. 'Ugly Row as Beauty Queen is Crowned,' *Independent*, 14 June 1988.
21. Olgin, 'Ten na korone'.
22. Kishchik, 'Faktor "iks" v vybore krasavitsy'.
23. I. Dzhafairova, 'Kazhdaya babinka-krasavitsa', *Bakinsky rabochy*, 12 July 1988.
24. Y. Savchenko, 'Miss Kolonia-90', *Kuranty*, 15 November 1990.
25. A. Kucherov, 'Queen Ivanova; or the Job which is not Respected', *Sputnik*, September 1990. (I am grateful to Elena Leonoff for drawing my attention to this article; the translation is hers.)
26. M. Parusnikova, '570 ocharovatelnykh debyutov', *Moskovsky komsomolets*, 19 April 1989.
27. G. Alimov, Yekaterina Chilichkina: moi ideal-Karmen', *Izvestiya*, 31 December 1988.
28. G. Alimov, 'Ya byla, tochno Alisa v strane chudes – govorit pervaya krasavitsa Moskvy Maria Kalinina', *Izvestiya*, 14 June 1988.
29. 'Miss Azia,' *Sovetskaya Belorussia*, 31 December 1988.
30. N. Kishchik, 'Miss Azia iz Alma-Aty',

31. 'Vnov priglashayutsya krasavitsy', *Sovetskaya Belorussia*, 25 August 1988.
32. Valentin Rasputin, 'Pravaya, levaya, gde storona?', *Nash sovremennik*, 1989, no. 11, pp. 140–9.
33. N. Rachkov, 'Nashi dukhovnye tsennosti: odna lyubov, odna zabota', *Pravda*, 13 May 1990.
34. T. Shcherbina, 'Tri temy yest na svete', Atmoda, 11 December 1989. For a discussion of the emerging sex industry, see Elizabeth Waters, 'Sex and Semiotic Confusion: Report from Moscow', *Australian Feminist Studies*, 1991, no. 12, pp. 1–14.
35. The BBC documentary 'Inside Story – Miss USSR' (20 September 1989) charted the course of the All-Union Beauty Contest from first round to final. Much of the information in the account that follows is taken from that source.
36. E. Tsirlin, 'Mesto vstrechi zasekrecheno', *Mokovskaya pravda*, 15 April 1989.
37. H. Shapiro, 'Here She Comes, Miss USSR!', *People's Weekly*, 25 September 1989.
38. T. Ivanova and S. Bugayev, 'Kto v Soyuze vsekh milee?', *Pravda Ukrainy*, 23 August 1988.
39. 'Kto v Soyuze vsekh milee?', *Sovetskaya Belorussia*, 1 August 1988.
40. B. Talov, 'Ekzamen dlya korolevy,' *Vechernaya Moskva*, 20 May 1989.
41. A. Chereshnev, 'Krepostnye korolevy?', *Pravda*, 24 June 1990.
42. 'A nu-ka devushki, a nu, krasavitsy!', *Golos rodiny*, January 1991, no. 3; V. Shirokova, 'Iz prelestnoi dyuzhiny,' *Moskovskaya pravda*, 3 January 1991.
43. K. Rotmanova, 'Miss Foto Baltic-90. Krasivo to, shto Bozhe', *Baltiyskoye vremya*, 8 January 1991.
44. 'Iz pribaltiyskoi – v Khelsinki', *Leningradskaya pravda*, 14 December 1990.
45. Richard Denton, 'Beauty and the Beasts', *The Listener*, 21 September 1989, p. 20.
46. Adrian Geiges, 'Chernukha, pornukha . . . ili seks v usloviakh razrukhi', *Novoye vremya*, October 1990, no. 44, p. 48.
47. See M. Molyneux, 'The "Woman Question" in the Age of Perestroika', *New Left Review*, 1990, no. 183, p. 31.
48. Interview with the author, February 1991.
49. Quoted in Denton, 'Beauty and the Beasts'.
50. See *Sobesednik*, March 1991, no. 11.
51. 'Konkurs krasoty v . . . KGB', *Kuranty*, 20 December 1990.
52. 'Primety vremeni', *Sovetskaya kultura*, 5 January 1991.

6

Sex and Young People

SERGEI GOLOD

This chapter is concerned with young people in the contemporary Soviet Union up to its dissolution in January 1992. A substantial amount of work exists on the 1920s in terms of analysis of empirical sociological material and theoretical discussion of sexuality's place in the culture of the time.[1] This work shows that researchers of the post-revolutionary period focused on only part of the spectrum of change, on what was readily visible owing to its 'explosive' nature. Profound structural changes remained beyond their field of vision. That is evidently why the fading of obvious interest in sex problems in the subsequent decade was perceived as a triumph for uniform 'collectivist' ideals. Yet one had only to look at selective surveys conducted in the mid-1960s among students and young white- and blue-collar workers to see a quite astonishing picture: age-old concepts of what was right and proper in sexual relationships had crumbled and the old idols came tumbling down. Emotions, it seemed, were poor counsellors; we needed to ponder on the facts and take an unbiased view of the whole panoply of motives, views, premises and ideals. Let us examine the trends consistently.

I made a survey of 500 students at ten Leningrad colleges in 1965. Among other things the young men and women were asked to indicate their attitude to pre-marital sex: 45 per cent approved, 33 per cent took a neutral position ('uncertain') and 22 per cent were against it. The bulk of students were therefore for pre-marital sex, while only one in five subscribed to the traditional view. Such findings obviously needed further confirmation. So seven years later I conducted a repeat survey of 500 students in the same colleges. The responses were as follows: 47 per cent approved, 39 per cent were neutral and 14 per cent were against. It seemed that I had sufficient grounds to conclude that the division was relatively stable.

135

Let me make a reservation. The approvers do not represent some monolithic aggregate: their positive orientation correlates with claims to satisfy a certain level of spiritual-emotional understanding. This assertion is based on the results of my testing 120 Leningrad factory- and office-workers in 1969 and 1970. Like the students, they were asked the question about whether pre-marital sexual was right but, additionally, they were asked if they thought it right in the context of three types of partner: a loved one, a boy or girlfriend and an acquaintance. No fewer than 90 per cent preferred such relationships with a loved one, over two thirds with a friend and almost 25 per cent with an acquaintance. So the great bulk of people, irrespective of gender, accept physical intimacy as a component part of loving relationships. The picture, however, is not as idyllic as it might seem: one in four respondents (more men than women) saw sexual contacts as attractive in themselves, outside the individual personality context.

Turning to an analysis of the evaluations, the correlation of responses undoubtedly depends on many factors, but my material suggests that two are overriding: the location (town or village) where people formed their moral values, and the ethnic group to which they belong. The first type of correlation is shown in Table 6.1. This provides evidence of an obvious difference: Leningraders had the maximum evaluation approving, the migrants were mostly uncertain. A comparison of polar judgements (along the vertical) provides a statistically meaningful preponderance of approval over condemnation among Leningraders and an almost even representation of condemnation and approval among the migrants. Apparently there are different value systems. V.G. Alexeyeva confirms this. She asked 300 Moscow schoolchildren and 300 migrant technical school students what they thought of 'intimate relations before marriage'. She found that 24 per cent of the students and 15 per cent of the schoolchildren were against ('no', 'never'), while 38 per cent and 56 per cent respectively were in favour ('in certain circumstances'). Her conclusion is that traditional values ('only marriage permits sexual intimacy') would seem to remain only among a few young people, and are more likely in technical school students than in school-children.[2]

Whether or not they are aware of it, it is certainly true that people from the countryside and small towns are still affected by authoritarian (patriarchal and religious) principles and direct social control from the family and the most immediate neighbouring environment. 'Village' morality helps preserve stringent stereotypes which operate

Table 6.1: Comparison of views of Leningraders and migrants in regard to pre-marital sex (percentages)*

Responses	Leningraders (students)	Migrants (workers)
Approve	55	24
Uncertain	34	50
Disapprove	11	26

Note: The sample is levelled out in regard to gender and age; the migrants were from villages and small towns
* Sample sizes: Leningraders 470; migrants 500

more or less effectively only in certain cultural-historical conditions. The tenacity of double standards is indicative in that respect. Among those moving from the village to the city, the 'approvers' constituted only 17 per cent of women and 33 per cent of men; the 'disapprovers' comprised 30 per cent and 20 per cent respectively. In the big city such standards show a marked dysfunctionality. Confirmation of that hypothesis is found in the shifting hierarchy of values among migrant factory workers. When they arrived in Leningrad 26 per cent were against pre-marital sex and only 24 per cent were in favour, but three years in the metropolis have their effect on changing values, not to mention their consistency: 30 per cent approved, 19 per cent disapproved.

A person who moves to a large town to take up permanent employment or studies alters more than her or his surroundings and cultural milieu; changes are also made to the inner perception of the world and to the individual lifestyle. To a large degree he or she adapts to a new ethos, to a complex internal system of social control. Strictly speaking, such people become accustomed to the diversity and changeability of surrounding phenomena, to the need to conduct themselves in a more productive and organised way; this produces greater toleration and breadth of views, a rational attitude to moral principles and independence in decision-making. Young men and women form new habits, interests and concepts; the need for spiritual and emotional collective experience encourages them to become part of the community and enhances the culture of their intellect and feelings.

Shifts in overall culture do not occur without some effect on sexual attitudes. At the same time, the fairly rapid adaptation of migrants in the big city is apparently due to the internalisation of cultural (including erotic-sexual) values taking place by degrees: by the penetration of thought processes and behavioural standards through mass media channels beyond one's own urbanised zone. The intensity of this mastering of new moral standards, however, depends on how easy it is to shake off patriarchal-authoritarian control. This is evident in a certain degree from the linkage between the moral standards of young workers and the place of residence of their parental families: those arriving in Leningrad from a small or medium-sized town showed the following set of values: 49 per cent were uncertain, 28 per cent approved and 23 per cent disapproved of pre-marital sex. Yet those who came from the countryside split thus: 50 per cent uncertain, 27 per cent disapproved and 23 per cent approved. In short, erstwhile towndwellers are more likely than young people brought up in the countryside to approve, and less likely to dis-approve, of sexual liaisons outside marriage. Roughly the same findings were produced by a survey of 4,000 students at 18 colleges in various parts of the country in 1978; they showed that 58 per cent of Leningraders, 50 per cent of regional centre residents, 47 per cent of those from other cities, 42 per cent of those from the capitals of certain republics (Belorussia, Russia and Turkmenia), 41 per cent of those from urban-type settlements and 35 per cent of rural inhabi-tants gave their seal of approval to pre-marital sex.

Ethnicity is the second layer of social influence on orientation structure. A survey of Yakuts held in 1974 at the Vilyuis Teacher Training College in Yakutia, northeastern Siberia, found that 272 of the students (73.5 per cent) were in favour of permitting pre-marital relations; 56 per cent of the young women (11.8 per cent of the sample) would agree if 'he and she respect each other'.[3] Four years later, in 1978, sociological research carried out among young rural and urban residents of the Ukrainian region of Chernovits found that 43.6 per cent of the men and 33.5 per cent of the women approved of sexual relations before marriage, while 53.5 per cent and 61 per cent respectively were against.[4] An interesting fact emerged from a 1985 survey in Lithuania, held to discover the attitude of urban and rural school-leavers (379 boys and 585 girls) to pre-marital sex. Some 47 per cent of the boys were in favour 'for themselves', but only 23 per cent of them approved of pre-marital sex 'for girls'. The female response was similar: only 10 per cent considered such relations permissible 'for themselves' and 22 per cent 'for boys'; while 46 per cent were against pre-marital sex 'for themselves' and 35 per cent were against it 'for boys'.[5] If we take another Baltic republic, Estonia, we find that during the 1970s seven out of ten male and two out of three female Estonians thought sexual relations before marriage 'natural'; four out of five men and women thought such behaviour 'natural' for their future spouses.[6]

To sum up attitudes to pre-marital sex, young people display a diversity of views. What is more, even one and the same assertion – say, of approval – conceals different perceptions of what relations between the sexes should be. For example, if we take the extreme positions, on the one hand love values are accentuated, on the other any need for prior conditions restricting sexual activity are rejected outright: 'If you want it, just do it.' The 'neutral' position is especially interesting. What does it actually mean? We have to remember that it is often produced by the marginal (in terms of age and residence) status of the respondents.

Restraining Sex Factors

For a fuller understanding of the moral content of sexual relationships we have to explain the factors that restrain young people from pre-marital sex. After all, rejection of such activity is also a positive action and, at the same time, a moral posture. Without fear of contradiction, we may say that if we were to ask cultural traditionalists what their principal inhibiting motive was, they would answer 'moral considerations', since uniform thinking is the mark of any authoritarian system. But what is the reality today? Does it differ substantially from that of the previous generation?

Empirical data reveal a multitude of factors that hamper unrestricted pre-marital sexual practices. The most popular, irrespective of the year of survey and the social background of respondents, continues to be morality (from 39 per cent of students in 1965 to 44 per cent of workers in 1974). Such a categorical assertion cannot be accepted without circumspection. When we turn to behaviour in practice we once again shed new light on the problem. It transpires that at the time the 1972 survey was taken more than 80 per cent of male students and almost 50 per cent of students had already had sexual experience (among the workers in 1969 and 1970 the corresponding figures were 86 per cent and 45 per cent). Is this not some kind of mass hypocrisy? That would be too facile and hasty an explanation; the material would seem to reflect a more complicated

picture. Apparently two regulating mechanisms are operating simultaneously, neither of which is fully tuned in so far as the action of one
is ineffective and the other is not yet running smoothly. We shall not
talk here of social regulation. But one thing is clear. In traditional
society, mores facilitated control over sexual behaviour: everyone
behaved in the same way, hence 'what should' happen coincided with
what did happen. According to those mores, sexual relations had to
be confined to marriage. Even today we find 'traces' of that principle
– more among women than men – but, at the same time, another type
of morality is coming into being. By its nature this is inherently
discordant with normative need and practice: thus people do not
always act as they are supposed to.

Let us note in passing that 'moral considerations' may mask other
motives for opposing pre-marital sex, such as lack of information,
inability to find a suitable partner, or lack of initiative or resolution in
making friends with the opposite sex. All other motives not only have
nothing to do with religious-patriarchal values, they are actually at
variance with them. Their only link is either with pragmatic considerations – a fear of exposure or infection, or (among female virgins)
psychophysiological problems – or with unformed sexual (but not
erotic) needs (reported by between 8 and 20 per cent). The most
marked factor is the futility of prohibitive morality in the light of such
restricting factors as 'lack of opportunity'. The simple fact is that
young people (more males than females) are prepared to overstep the
traditional mark; they do so, without giving it a thought, as soon as
the right opportunity presents itself. All they need is suitable living
conditions.

We cannot ignore the relative importance of the motive of 'fear of
possible consequences' (reported by 10–14 per cent). What possible
consequences do young people fear? Reproach from relatives or
friends? By no means. They are scared of unwanted pregnancies.
This once again confirms the lack of elementary knowledge about the
physiology of sex, demonstrated in this fragment of a letter sent to a
Leningrad family advice bureau:

> We've been married a couple of months . . . Happy. We've come
> to you for advice. Would you please tell us exactly when and how
> one gets pregnant? We need to know because we have absolutely
> no idea (we just didn't need to know before) 'what' and 'how'.

Let us now look at what lies behind 'other' restraining factors (cited by about 5 per cent). Respondents confined themselves to two forms of motivation here: 'fear of starting sex' and 'absence of a loved one'. Some young people who have heard scare stories about sex from their peers (research shows that it is precisely peers who are the first to provide 'enlightenment') do all they can to avoid it, frightened or disgracing themselves in a woman's (or man's) eyes. Even if such people do attempt to go through with the sexual act, it may well end in disaster. And, having experienced failure, as the sexopathologist N.V. Ivanov has justly said, a man finds a way of reconciling himself to the situation by rejecting any genital intimacy, yet retaining a 'petting' option, thereby obtaining a certain degree of satisfaction while being relieved of responsibility.[7] Figuratively speaking, the unwillingness of some men to take on any obligations has reached into the bedroom. Women sometimes have a similar complex under the impact of a Victorian upbringing, whose message is that physical relations are vile, dirty and exclusively reserved for men, while women are meant to preserve their purity if they do not wish to descend to such depths of depravity.

The second of these observed motives ('absence of a loved one') is symptomatic. It reveals the development and intensification of a new moral foundation to sexual relations – a spiritual-emotional involvement. More precisely, love is now looked upon by some young people as a great personal value.

There is no ground for doubting the connection between factors restraining young people from sexual relations and their views on the acceptability of the same. Despite the fact that the major restraining factors are identical in all three student aggregates, their relative importance depends on the type of orientation. For example, 'moral considerations' are a greater factor for disapprovers than for approvers. A comparison of students and workers reveals that 'moral considerations' are always cited as a restraining factor, although, as mentioned earlier, this expression has a myriad meanings. For workers who reject sexual autonomy, it evidently signifies the view that all extra-marital contacts without exception are amoral; while students who approve such contacts may use the term to signify the 'lack of a loved one'. Further, the traditional stereotypes of thinking play less of a role in all student samples than in those of workers; on the other hand, students find it more difficult 'to arrange' what they regard as a suitable 'opportunity'. This once again indicates the fairly high level of students' claims of sexual contacts. It is perfectly logical for young people (who approve of pre-marital sexual relations) to

point to 'lack of opportunity' and 'sexual need' as restraining factors
(as 45 per cent of them do). At the same time, between a third and
half of the disapprovers and those who could not define their position
indicated the same factors. In conclusion, let us note that workers
who disfavour sexual activity are constrained by 'fear of the consequences' and 'lack of sexual need' (22 per cent), which are motives in
no way determined by a person's ethics.

Motives for Sexual Intercourse

It is now time to reveal the place of motives and practice in the study
of sexual intercourse, in as much as people's actions are the best
embodiment of their thoughts. Specific testimony to orientations and
actual behaviour enables us to find measures to harmonise them –
that is, to bring about a unity of the elements of moral awareness and
practical activity.

Let us note that 69 per cent of the students and 70 per cent of the
workers who were inclined (in the 1965 and 1972 surveys) to approve
of sexual contacts outside marriage had had such experience themselves. In a word, young men and women approving of pre-marital
sex overwhelmingly put their approval into practice. Without a doubt
it is the position of the 'disapprovers' that is a paradox, since about
half of them have had sexual experience. One thing is clear: there are
no grounds to doubt that sexual activity increases as people depart
from the fixed stereotypes of traditional thinking. That is apparent
from the findings of surveys of persons with higher education
(doctors, teachers, lecturers and cultural figures), 205 of whom were
questioned in 1969 and 250 in 1989.

The 1969 survey showed that 88 per cent who approved of pre-
marital sex had actually had sexual experience; the respective figures
for the disapprovers and waverers were 76 per cent and 46 per cent.
In the 1989 survey the shares were distributed as follows: 92 per cent,
59 per cent and 70 per cent. The only meaningful difference between
words and deeds would seem to be with persons who are against pre-
marital sex. The behavioural differences between students and the
professional group may be explained in various ways. One thing,
however, is certain. Most students are unmarried, so the potential
exists for them to put their desires into practice. On the other hand,
all the surveyed men and women with higher education were
married, so they were looking back on past history; the evaluations

Table 6.2: The age at which students and people with a higher education begin their sex lives, by year of survey (as a percentage of the total number who have had sexual experience)

Age at first sex experience	Students		Professional people	
	1965	1972	1969	1989
Under 16	5.3	8.2	3.4	5.6
16–18	33.0	30.8	14.6	24.4
19–21	39.5	43.8	35.6	44.0
22–24	19.5	16.0	32.7	20.0
Over 24	2.7	1.2	13.7	7.0

bear a largely academic character. What is striking, however, is that level of education affects the degree of critical perception of moral principles 'prescribed' by traditional society. What does that mean in practice? If we use a test that differentiates the potential partner, we find that some 80 per cent of men with secondary education think it possible 'for themselves' to have sexual intercourse with 'any woman', about a third with their 'girlfriends' and almost two thirds with 'an acquaintance'. About the same number of women with a secondary education (80 per cent) reserve the possibility of sex with a 'loved one' for themselves, while one in ten think it acceptable with a 'boyfriend' or an 'acquaintance'. For men and women with higher education the respective figures were 100 per cent, 27 per cent and 5 per cent. We might risk a cautious preliminary hypothesis: the empirical evidence testifies not to a decline in sexual contacts among young people but rather to their qualitative transformation. One would hope that characteristics of sexual intercourse – the age at which it starts, the motives and type of partner involved – might help us to explain this fairly ambiguous situation.

Let us begin our analysis with the age at which people have their first sexual experience. Even a quick glance at Table 6.2 is enough to indicate certain trends. First is the growth in the number of people beginning their sex lives at an early age (up to 19) and, conversely, a diminution of those having their first sexual experiences when they were older (after 24).

Differences in the intensity of this process are discernible among students and professional people. These differences are associated more with the interval between surveys than with the social status of the respondents. In short, the greater the timelag the more discernible the trend. There was in fact only a 1 per cent increase in the number of students having sex before the age of 18, while the number of professionals in this group rose 12 points over the 20 years. The modal group (19–21 years) increased by 4 per cent and 8 per cent respectively.

If we seek other comparisons we see that the professionals surveyed in 1969 mainly entered into their first sexual union while they were students – that is, roughly in the first part of the 1950s. We can therefore understand their relatively small involvement in pre-marital sex before they came of age and, conversely, their active involvement after the age of 22. These were the years when double standards prevailed, nourished by the external preference for collec-tivist values and asceticism. The professional people represented in the second survey were at college somewhere in the early 1970s. What is patently obvious is that their behaviour is not identical to that of the students who were directly interviewed in 1972. Why is that? Firstly, among the students the proportion of those from the countryside and small towns is substantially lower than in the group representing people with higher education. But that is not all. We must also bear in mind a particular trait of the surveys. In the professional group of 1989, men and women were equally repre-sented, while the 1972 student group was clearly weighted in favour of men. This tells us a good deal. Men, as we shall see below, begin sex earlier and are more intensively involved.

It would be wrong to think that the age at which sex life begins in itself presupposes a particular quality of relationships between a man and a woman, although it would also be fallacious to ignore its influence completely. The lowering of the sexual-experience age limit is not so much due to accelerated physical development in the twentieth century as to incomplete erotic maturation – the unformed spiritual structure of the personality. Let us take one example. When a 15 year-old girl writes to a well-known youth newspaper, fervently justifying casual sex because of her irresistible longing for men, her actions are not purely instinctive but depend upon society, her immediate surroundings and the influence of primitive culture. The latter remark will become clearer as we elucidate the motives and object of the first intimacy. Let us examine the motives first (see Table 6.3).

It is clear that three motives characterise the behaviour of most young people. The hierarchy of preferences in Table 6.3 reflects not only the formal (quantitative) aspect of such relationships but also

Table 6.3: Motives for engaging in one's first sexual act, comparing the social background of respondents (as a percentage by survey year)*

Motives	Students		Workers	Professionals	
	1965	*1972*	*1974*	*1965*	*1989*
Love	41.7	35.8	36.7	50.5	42.0
Sexual desire	33.7	32.4	28.4	27.5	47.2
Curiosity	30.9	22.9	18.7	17.2	19.2
Seduction	11.1	7.0	9.3	7.4	6.8
Chance affair	9.0	13.5	12.1	4.9	7.6
Other motives	1.2	0.3	0.6	–	11.6
Can't say	–	–	–	–	1.8

Note: Respondents could select one or two motives
* Sample sizes: students, 339 in 1965, 331 in 1972; workers, 334; professionals, 205 in 1965, 250 in 1989

their very essence. In all groups surveyed (with the exception of the professional people in the 1989 survey), the principal motivation coincides – no fewer than a third of respondents said that they achieved full feelings of love in sexual intercourse. It does not take much foresight to know that women predominated in this group; the 1969 survey (in which one in two stressed 'love') was asymmetrical in favour of women. The second motive ('sexual desire') would seem to speak for itself, but it is not as neat and tidy as it seems. For men and women this concept has a broad semantic range: from love-filled passion to physiological relaxation. If we turn our attention to the 1989 group we are bound to ask how can we explain the dominant position of the 'sexual desire' factor. Bearing in mind that there were an equal number of men and women in the sample group, it would be wrong to ascribe this motivation simply to gender differences. Rather, we are dealing here with a rationalisation of past experience. After all, for all the professionals the first experience of sex was in the past, as much as ten or 15 years earlier, so they were more qualified to judge objectively what their motivation had been.

The third leading motive was 'curiosity'. Its parameters are well defined (18–30 per cent) and, in all probability, reflect the realities of sexual culture. The fact that people do enter into sex with a 'cognitive' goal, even though social institutions choose to deny this, just goes to show how those institutions have ignored an aspect of everyday life and, at the same time, have generally shown contempt for the world of the individual.

The significant representation (I would stress that, since anomie is apparently a constant companion of civilisation) of unspecified erotic motives (seduction, chance affairs and so on) in all social strata is eloquent testimony to the spiritual state of our culture.

Any one particular motive depends on the age of first involvement in sex, as is evident from the professional group. 'Sexual desire' was the major motivation for people under 18, while 'love' was the main reason for the 19–20 year-olds. The number of 'curious' respondents narrowed with age: while in 1969 'curiosity' was present in the lowest age group and, to some extent, in the 19–21 group, it was exclusively a teenage factor in the 1989 group. As far as other motives are concerned, they existed in more or less stable proportions. For example, 'chance' relations primarily characterised the behaviour of the under-16s, although they were not entirely ignored by the 19–21s.

Figuratively speaking, we should put the finishing touches to the object of desire when completing our description of young people's sexual behaviour. The choice of a partner, one might suppose, is very much connected with the respondent's age and intimacy motive. What did the surveys show?

A statistical analysis carried out on five surveys (students, 1965, 1972; workers, 1974; professionals, 1969 and 1989) revealed a certain correlation of partner choice with the age of the respondent. This may be roughly expressed as follows: up to the age of 16 almost 60 per cent of respondents began their sex lives with a girl or boyfriend, another 30 per cent with someone considerably older and preferably from a different sociocultural background, while the rest had their first experience with someone from a different sociomarital status. A significant shift takes place in the next age band (16–18). Much the same proportion described their first partner as a girl/boyfriend, while the percentage citing an older person fell by a third and the next category of partners comprised brides or husbands-to-be – virtually one in ten of respondents. With the 19–21 year olds, the position with the girl or boyfriend was fairly stable, second place was now taken by the bride or husband-to-be, while 'a man or woman considerably older' came third with 20 per cent. Finally, by the age of 22–24 young people's first sexual partners fell into the following groups: wife or husband; bride- or husband-to-be; girl or boyfriend. We must make one reservation. It has to be remembered that any name is only a handle, not the essence of the phenomenon being analysed. Different people use the same words to mean different things. For example, what meaning is given to the concept of 'boy or girlfriend'? For 14 or

15 year-old girls it could be 'my guy' or the local 'daredevil', but for a 19 year-old boy what may seem more important is the girl's subcultural sexual specificity, her erotic-sexual worth. We can establish a close link between the type of partner and motives for sexual intercourse. For the sake of simplicity let us confine ourselves to the professional group. On the one hand, the student (and even the worker) surveys do not provide us with one iota of new information; on the other, the professionals were interviewed at an interval of 20 years, so they give us a wide perspective. What do we find here?

Those respondents who justified their first sexual relations as fulfilling feelings of love categorised their first partners thus: wife or husband (33–41 per cent), bride- or husband-to-be (24–35 per cent) and girl or boyfriend (17–20 per cent). Among those who associated their first sexual activity with sexual desire, the first partners were described as follows: girl or boyfriend (50–55 per cent), a considerably older woman or man (18 per cent), and bride or husband-to-be or wife or husband (10–18 per cent). The 'curious' formally reiterated the previous order, but with a lower quantitative representation of wives/husbands and girl/boyfriends and, conversely, nominating 'chance affairs' twice as often. Other motives are statistically insignificant, but if we take one of them – 'seduction' – for the sake of general orientation and ask who is the major seducer? The principal answer (not hard to guess) is 'a man or woman considerably older' (up to 40 per cent said this), followed by 'a married man or woman' and, sometimes, however odd it may seem, the 'husband-to-be'.

Satisfaction with Sexual Relationships

There is no reason to doubt that the empirical material presents a true picture of young people's erotic-sexual behaviour over the last 30–40 years. This in itself is a substantial advance in understanding a slice of real life; moreover, it has made it possible to take the next step: placing the analysed relationships into the general context of culture. However, that brings us up against a whole series of problems, the principal of which is finding an adequate norm criterion. Researchers are cautious about falling into the danger of moralising. After all, if we fall back on Christian-patriarchal principles what we have found only goes to show how boundlessly sinful young people are! We recall that such a state of affairs was noted in

Russia at the turn of the century and again in the 1920s. We seem to be moving full circle. Yet we could look at matters differently: behaviour is changing logically, but the criteria are out of date and no longer meet the new realities.

The nineteenth-century Russian philosopher Vladimir Solovyov detected a crisis of 'naturalness' – meaning marital procreation as a criterion determining the morality of sexual self-expression. This criterion has long since ceased to reflect the essence of sexual relations and only ascribes the formal limits of their morality in an authoritarian way: marriage is marriage. The criterion we need should reflect the qualitative state of mutual relations between the genders; in particular, it should show the extent to which natural relations have become human relations. This indicator can easily be in the form of a continuous scale which shows particular correlations, let us say, in regard to growing alienation between the spiritual 'top' and the material-corporeal 'bottom'.

An individual's satisfaction with sexual relationships is closely linked to the degree of spiritual-emotional involvement, to the depth and brightness of feelings. At the instrumental level, 'spiritual-emotional involvement' is seen as a combination of three components: expressiveness, selectivity and moral integrity (unity of disposition and behaviour). No characteristics of relations linked to one's job, social status, ethnic group, age or marital status can, in our view, vie with the yardstick of spiritual-emotional involvement when we refer to their moral basis and evaluation. It goes without saying, of course, that specific indicators in particular and in each individual instance may not express the true meaning of relations. But in questioning a large number of people we may never the less suggest that a chance affair combined with its negative evaluation and dissonance in the social status and cultural needs of partners normally points to alienation of relationships; conversely, a love motivation for an affair in combination with its approval and harmony of cultural interests between the partners testifies to the presence of spiritual-emotional involvement. Motivation for entering into sexual relations, together with the partner-type, enable us to determine the extent of self-justification for young people's sexual relationships in the light of social prescriptions and standards; a negative evaluation of pre-marital relations by a person who none the less practises them must indicate the absence of expressiveness and selectivity, while a positive evaluation to a lesser extent shows a harmony of moral position and behaviour.

We were able to construct four types of relationships by combining the parameters described. The first is 'love'. Sexual contacts here are generally self-justified; love is the motive for intercourse, a 'girl or boyfriend', or 'bride- or husband-to-be' is the partner. Love is understood as a striving for the moral-aesthetic ideal, combining with a natural desire for a particular person and physical intimacy with that person. This behaviour provides true intimacy, erotic accord and bodily harmony. In other words, natural here become human relations, and human become natural relations.

The second type of relationships is 'standard'. This is statistically modal. Sexual relationships are largely seen as justified by the individual concerned. The major motive for having intercourse is sexual desire, and occasionally self-assertion and curiosity. One normally chooses a girl or boyfriend as partner, someone close in cultural needs and sociomarital status. We should distinguish two tendencies in the formation of this type. The first comes from the socioeconomic and moral emancipation of women, and also the extension of the bounds of sexual subculture; as a result there has been an erosion of the double standard and therefore an increasing number of young women are entering into sexual unions. The second tendency is that sexual intercourse is being based on certain typical patterns that show regular, often superficial emotional experiences. At that level sexuality has become a form of personal communication (recreation), where relations, given all their possible constancy and stability, even sometimes spiritual depth, are not marked by vivid expression and strong feelings. The formation of 'standard' relations results from the development of mass communications, the greater mobility of young people, the anonymity of behaviour in large cities and the influence on individual consciousness of the same patterns of behaviour through film, TV and press channels.

The third type is the 'stereotype'. Respondents here frequently justify such sexual relations, but more rarely give any concerted view. Curiosity or seduction, more rarely sexual desire, serve as motives for sex. As a rule, the partner is a person with different cultural needs and social status, although one cannot fully preclude contacts with an individual of the same socialmarital status (especially in regard to adolescents). The stereotype form largely presupposes maximally alienated contacts (see below), although it does have other specific traits. In the first place there is selectivity of the object, although this is a stereotype and not an emotional-aesthetic embellishment. What does stereotype selectivity mean? During the sexual maturation period young boys and girls develop an image of the physical ideal in regard to men and women. Subsequently, there is a less than fully realised identification of the real object with the ideal. For sexual union to occur, we need a certain everyday situation as well as a person who conforms to the stereotype. People who enter into such relationships substantially show a spiritual emptiness and emotional lack of response. Even though the paramount latent expectation is one of enjoyment, the actual contacts take the form of crude sensuality: the cult of the body is not accompanied by any expressiveness and eros is not the individual's inner need.

The fourth type is 'depravity'. Young men and women drawn into such liaisons are emotionally immature, do not express any selectivity and their primitive motivation for intimacy is curiosity and casual sex. Individuals entering into maximally alienated affairs have numerous contacts and therefore know virtually nothing (nor do they want to know anything) about their partners. To illustrate the nature of such contacts, we give an extract from an interview we conducted in an infectious diseases clinic.

The patient L. came to the clinic in October 1969 with recurring gonorrhoea. She was 19 and a technical college student. Externally she was quite attractive and extremely shy. She smoked and drank (preferring champagne and cognac). She had had her first sexual contact in May of the previous year, since when she had had between eight and nine partners. She described her first experience as follows. That evening she had been to a concert with a female friend; afterwards she had struck up an acquaintance with a member of the orchestra who had given her his telephone number. She had spent the night with her friend and next morning 'found' the number and telephoned the hotel where the man was staying. They met, had a few drinks and went to bed. She said she had not wanted to, had even warned her partner of her virginity. He had calmed her by promising he would not 'go that far'. She had gained no pleasure from intercourse. Further contacts were at the same emotional level. When asked why, then, she had such sexual contacts when they gave her no satisfaction, she replied that she did it 'for company's sake'; 'I have to do something with myself'. She did not regard her conduct as in any way immoral. When asked whether she would join a brothel, she indignantly insisted she was not that sort of girl.

Maximally alienated sexual contacts are caused by a lack of internal responsibility, moral degradation and cultural primitivism. Any attempt to use physical intimacy to resolve the problem of psychological and everyday instability, to find a solution to social isolation without investing a modicum of feelings into intercourse is doomed to failure. Depraved relations may provide a shortlived release from the 'prison' of loneliness through creating the illusion of unity. It is not so in reality, for only personal intercourse encourages true unity. The encounter between 'two bodies' intensifies the state of loneliness. The physiology and psychology of depravity are based on transforming sexuality into a means rather than an end; in other words, it confines interest in the other person to their role in the sexual act. It is using the partner as a means to attain one's goal. Depravity exists where sexual relations between men and women are not based on selectivity.

Such a classification outlines only the principal types of young people's sexual behaviour. In practice we meet a far greater variety. Moreover, sexual liaisons are capable of evolution: 'love' intercourse may be transformed into 'standard', and vice versa. It is even possible to combine the two, but never to combine the 'love' or 'standard' with the 'stereotype' or 'depraved' type, since the first two presuppose a personal level of intercourse and the latter pair totally exclude it.

References

1. See Sergei Golod, 'Izuchenie polovoi morali v 20-ye gody', *Sotsiologicheskie issledovaniya*, 1986, no. 2, pp. 152–5; Sergei Golod, 'Voprosy semi i polovoi morali v diskussiyakh 20-kh godov', *Marxistskaya eticheskaya mysl v SSSR (20-ye – pervaya polovina 30-kh godov)* (Moscow: 1989), pp. 244–68.
2. V.G. Alexeyeva, 'Neformalnye gruppy podrostkov v usloviyakh goroda', *Sotsiologicheskie issledovaniya*, 1977, no. 3.
3. B.N. Popov, 'Otnoshenie molodyozhi k voprosam lyubvi, braka i semi', *Selskaya molodyozh Yakutii* (Yakutsk: 1969).
4. D.E. Nemirovsky, 'Ob otnoshenii molodyozhi k dobrachnoi polovoi zhizni', *Sotiologicheskie issledovaniya*, 1982, no. 1.
5. G. Navaitis, 'Otnoshenie molodyozhi k dobrachnym polovym svyazam', *Sotsiologicheskie issledovaniya*, 1988, no. 2.
6. A. Tavit and H. Kadastik, 'Nachalo sexualnoi zhizni', *Problemy stabilnosti braka. Problemy semi* (Tartu: 1980), pp. 70–4.
7. N.V. Ivanov, 'Znachimost uchota otnosheniy k bolezni pri psikhoterapii funktsionalnykh sexualnykh rasstroistv', *Aktualnye voprosy sexopatologii* (Moscow: 1967).

7

Medical Sexology

LEV SHCHEGLOV

By medical sexology (sexopathology) we mean 'the area of clinical medicine that studies functional aspects of sexual disorders, including behavioural, personal and social.'[1] Medical sexology is a part of general sexology which Igor Kon defines as that 'area of knowledge that comprehensively studies social and psychological aspects of relations between the sexes, and the physiology and pathology of life'.[2] Any definition of the place of medical sexology in relation to other disciplines goes beyond theory and directly impinges on the practice of treatment. Despite sexology being recognised in recent years as being 'autonomous', differing views exist here and abroad on the appropriateness of that autonomy and its limits.

History

Russian medical sexology at the turn of the century typically took an encyclopedic approach to studying sexual disorders, providing for a weakening in straightforward biological determination in favour of sociopsychological mechanisms. At the instigation of medical circles in St Petersburg, Moscow and Kiev, publications by many authors began to appear in the mid-nineteenth century; the trouble was that they all referred merely to statistical questions on age of sexual maturation, entry into marriage, the climacteric period and factors affecting their earlier or later manifestation.

Several eminent Russian physiologists engaged in research into sexuality, including the physiologists I.R. Tarkhanov (1885)[3] and A.A. Ukhtomsky (1923)[4], and the doctors V.M. Bekhterev (1914)[5], I.I. Mechnikov (1913) and V.M. Tarnovsky (1886).[6] In 1904 A. Nenadovich read a report to the obstetrics and female diseases section of the Pirogov Doctors' Congress in St Petersburg, in which he classified the various forms of female frigidity in order to pinpoint their causes. This was the first time this had been done in Russia. The works of the Russian sexologist-encyclopedist L.Y. Yakobzon (1915, 1918, 1927 and 1928) are also particularly worthy of mention; many of them retain their relevance even today.[7]

The eve of the first Russian Revolution (1905) saw mounting interest in the individual and his/her needs, bringing a revision of established social norms and concepts, including in regard to sexual mores. The first 'sex census' among Moscow students was carried out in 1903 and 1904, but the results did not see light of day until a few years later.[8] Sociological research into sexology continued up to the beginning of the 1930s, after which time no sociological-statistical research took place for many years to come. It was only in 1969 that I.A. Popov's dissertation brought Soviet sexopathology back to a study of the statistical material.[9]

The development and the peculiarities of Russian and Soviet sexopathology are reflected in the publication of scholarly literature. The Saltykov-Shchedrin State Public Library in Leningrad (now renamed St Petersburg) has some 1,500 items in the discipline from the late eighteenth century up to the present day. Table 7.1 presents an analysis of these works by year of publication. Most of the books published before 1917 are Russian translations of foreign works. The table shows a large number of publications between 1917 and the 1930s, then an almost complete lull up to the early 1960s, and a new surge thereafter. This process reflects the overall climate in the country.

The three principal approaches to medical sexology – monodisciplinary, multidisciplinary and interdisciplinary – are all reasonably represented in Soviet sexopathology. With the monodisciplinary approach, sexual dysfunction is made dependent on a traditional medical division (a urologist or a psychiatrist, for example treats a case of sexual pathology in isolation from other specialists). Most Soviet experts today believe that it is wrong to deal with a patient in this way, in so far as it precludes an integrated approach to the problem. Second, the multidisciplinary approach is a comprehensive way of conceptualising the treatment of the sexually sick, when 'brigade' aid is offered to the patient – that is, from doctors of different specialities simultaneously. Despite the formally multi-profile approach, however, it is unable adequately to evaluate sexual disorders and, consequently, to treat them successfully. Finally,

Table 7.1: Analysis of works published on sexopathology from the late eighteenth century up to 1990

Subject matter	Year of publication					
	up to 1917	1917–36	1956–60	1961–9	1970–80	after 1980
Male sexual disorders	15	4	3	4	25	12
Aetiology and pathogenesis of sexual disorders	–	1	–	–	8	10
Masturbation	31	23	–	–	–	–
Priapism	5	–	–	–	–	–
Impotence	53	22	–	7	14	–
Aetiology and pathogenesis of sexual disorders	2	1	2	–	–	–
Treatment of sexual disorders	13	1	–	3	12	3
Sexual hygiene	145	62[a]	n.a.	7	13[b]	6

Note: a = 1917–30, b = 1970–3

presentday Soviet sexopathology is capable of constructing a model of interdisciplinary sexology, thereby opening up a new stage in its development.

Attempts to improve the training of doctors in sexopathology were made long before official recognition of the specialism. A national seminar on training sexopathology doctors, under the stewardship of Professor N.V. Ivanov, was first held in Gorky (now Nizhny Novgorod) in 1963. The seminar was the result of the enthusiasm of its participants, doctors from varying disciplines interested in problems of sexology and sexopathology; it was the first proclamation of the future scientific discipline and specialist health service in the country. Subsequently similar seminars were held in Gorky during 1964 and 1966. The 1967 seminar was held in the Sexopathology Unit of the Moscow Psychiatry Research Institute of the Russian Federation Health Ministry. From 1973 the Unit has functioned as the Soviet Research Centre on Sexopathology, coordinating the activities of sexopathologists throughout the country.

In 1977 Igor Kon gave a lecture on interdisciplinary aspects of sexology for psychiatrists, psychologists and sexopathologists; this was at the V.M. Bekhterev Psychoneurological Institute in Leningrad. The material was subsequently published in Kon's book *Vvedenie v sexologiyu* (*Introduction to Sexology*),[10] which is today the vade-mecum for sexologists and sexopathologists in what was the USSR.

During the 1970s the country was taking its first steps in organising a sexological service. Patients suffering from sexual disorders were being given advice and treatment in virtually all 15 union republican capitals and the major cities. At the same time, a tiny amount of research was being undertaken in a fairly chaotic and disparate way, there was no back-up training for specialist doctors and the forms of organisation of the sexological service varied considerably, consisting of sexopathological clinics, Marriage and Family advice bureaux, medical-psychological advice units, family guidance clinics and so on. The standard ratio proposed by the USSR Health Minister of one doctor for every million people was patently inadequate.

At that time some areas of the country began to display initiative and independence in organising and promoting their own sexological service. For example, for several years Rostov has tried to establish a specific morphological approach to sexological problems; a urological aspect of sexology is being worked out in the Ukraine under the auspices of the Sexopathology Centre of the Kiev Urology and Nephrology Research Institute. A monthly seminar for improving the qualifications of sexologist doctors and medics from different disciplines concerned with sexopathology has been meeting in Leningrad since 1980. In the same city, S.S. Libikh (of the Institute for Doctor Training) has been running informal seminars for psychologists, psychotherapists and sexologists since 1976. These envisage more than reports on particular themes, and includes reference to specific cases from clinical practice and broad debate.

The All-Union Scientific Method Centre on Sexopathological Issues headed by G.S. Vasilchenko in Moscow is working on a system of structural analysis of sexual disorders, representing an aggregate of methods used for assessing a sexual disorder as a whole and locating the causes and mechanisms of the illness. The Centre is also compiling a pathogenetic classification of potential disorders, holding statistical investigations and drawing together the clinical experience of sexopathologist practitioners. For several years it has, moreover, provided training for probationer doctors from various cities and republics.

The publishers *Meditsina* put out a textbook for doctors, entitled *General Sexopathology*, in 1977,[11] and *Personal Sexopathology*, edited by G.S. Vasilchenko, in 1983.[12] In spite of a certain academic slant and difficulties in practical application of the ideas proposed,

Sex and Russian Society

both books played a large part in promoting the clinical thinking of sexopathology doctors.

The Moscow Psychiatry Research Institute, where the All-Union Centre for Sexopathology Issues was located, published in 1967 the collection *Aktualnye voprosy sexopatologii* (*Important Issues of Sexopathology*),[13] which was the first publication to offer Soviet readers an extensive spectrum of research and the practical experience of practising doctors. The next two monographs, *Voprosy sexopatologii* (*Sexopathological Issues*)[14], 1969, and *Problemy sovremennoi sexopatologii* (*Problems of Contemporary Sexopathology*)[15], 1972, were very much in the same vein. They filled a void in scientific information for a large number of doctors. For sexopathologists of the 1970s such publications were invaluable as both guides and reference books.

In the early 1970s the country's first family guidance bureau, headed by A.M. Svyadoshch, came into being in Leningrad. One distinguishing feature of the bureau was the wide range of specialists it had on hand: sexopathologists, psychotherapists, psychologists, lawyers and gynaecologists. It offered its services to any person who wished to consult it from anywhere in the country. The service was bedevilled by many difficulties and official lack of understanding of tasks and goals.

Female Sex Problems

A milestone in the development of Soviet sexopathology was the appearance of Svyadoshch's *Zhenskaya sexopatologiya* (*Female Sexopathology*) in 1974, which immediately became a bestseller and subsequently ran to three editions.[16]

Female sexology and sexopathology gained momentum through the energy and enthusiasm of a small handful of researchers. The first Russian work on female sexopathology was Tarnovsky's article 'Izvrashchenie polovovo chuvstva u zhenshchin' ('Perversion of Sexual Feelings among Women'), published in 1895.[17] In 1904 Nenadovich gave the first ever report on female sexual frigidity (see above). In the early 1920s books on female sexuality by foreign (Hammond, Calverton, Lindsey, Roleder) and Soviet authors (Gelman, Golosovker, Gurevich, Grosser, Zdravomyslov, Mandalshtam, Yakobzon) were published. After the brief blossoming of Soviet sexology and sexopathology there ensued a protracted period of hypocrisy and displacement of such sciences from the public and individual mind. This process applied especially to female sexology, in as much as the notion of primordial female asexuality and non-involvement in all things carnal was implanted in the mass psyche. The education of young girls took on a puritanical air, sexological problems were ascribed to men only and research and publications were set back several decades.

The restoration stage in Soviet sexology, dating from the late 1960s, applied less to research into female sexuality. For about 20 years, from the late 1960s until the late 1980s, a paltry two books and five articles saw the light of day. Only ten papers at the first conference on sexopathology, held in Moscow in 1968, were on female sexuality, while more than 50 were on male sexopathology. Interestingly enough, the trend was even more marked in the 1980s against the background of an overall upsurge in the discipline: female sexopathology attracted just a single paper out of all three conferences held in 1981, 1984 and 1985.

Understandably, the same processes were at work in medical practice, with the sex advice bureaux being basically concerned with male sexual problems. According to several authors, the percentage of women among the patients of sexopathologist doctors varies from 1 per cent to 10 per cent, and most of those are invited for consultation in connection with their husband's or partner's sexual problems. The principal motive for women to turn to a sexopathology doctor is lack of sexual satisfaction – up to 75.3 per cent of the total number of patients (according to data of the Sexological Clinic's Medical Unit attached to the Obstetrics and Gynaecological Institute in Leningrad from 1976 to 1985). Many women who have sexual problems suffer serious neurosis and depression, and even attempt suicide, yet the socially conditioned shame that women bear stops them from seeing a specialist.

In recent years there has been a small but steady rise in women visiting sexopathologists. Women's sexual behaviour is increasingly recognised as important to the sexual compatibility of partners.

Love and Marriage

A veritable revolution in the institution of marriage and the family seems to be taking place in the country.[18] The transformation in the presentday family has gone a long way; we are seeing a transition from the multigeneration family to the single- or two-generation family, a falling birth rate and general rise in the divorce rate, an increase in sociopsychological disharmony and lack of adaptation in family relationships, a change in family values and decline in the family's importance as an education unit. Young people show a lack of readiness for marriage in all spheres – sociopsychological, material, sexual and so on.

Research into motives for marriage, carried out in the 1960s and 1970s by A.G. Kharchev and published in 1979, points to love as the chief motivating factor for 85–90 per cent of all marriage unions. In 1987 L.Y. Gozman described two basic models of love.[19] The first, the 'pessimistic' model, is set by the individual's dependence on the object of love and the link between love and negative emotions (fear of losing the love of the object of one's love, fear of losing one's beloved). This love model makes a person dependent, maintains a constant level of concern and hampers personality development. In its extreme form the model may cause a nervous breakdown and such marriages frequently translate marital partnership into pseudo-partnership, rivalry or isolation.

The second, the 'optimistic' model, is characterised by dependence on the object of love, while retaining a positive reason for contact; it develops against a background of psychological comfort and facilitates the personality development of both spouses.

Sex Education

The problems of sex education and upbringing also bear a specific Soviet imprint. A sex education system as such is practically non-existent. By decision of the USSR Education Ministry a new course was introduced into schools in 1983: 'hygiene and sex education' for 15 year-olds (twelve hours during the school year) and 'ethics and psychology of family life' for 16 and 17 year-olds (34 hours a year). Formally, sex education in schools is compulsory and universal, but in practice almost nothing of what is taught within the recommended curriculum corresponds to either the principles or the goals of sex education. There are two overriding reasons for this.

The first is the repressive, moralising attitude to sexuality. To a large degree this phenomenon comes from age-old prejudices; a person's sexuality is regarded as something 'dirty' and forbidden, and the idea is widespread that it is harmful to have an open and frank discussion of sexual problems. Secondly, there is a lack of professional educators. What we need is 'education of the educators'. The absence of sex literacy among educators often precludes any adequate response to problems posed, which reduces sex education in schools to naught. It is no less easy for parents to surmount the barriers erected by the education they themselves received. Bearing in mind the psychological specifics of adolescent age, when parents and pedagogues are often excluded from the adolescent's reference group, one has to agree with D.N. Isayev and V.Y. Kagan that doctors should be the central figures in arranging sex education.[20]

Sex education could be organised through the consecutive implementation of three stages:

- sex education of the educators
- sex education of parents (the adult population)
- sex education of children and adolescents

The gaps in preparing children and adolescents for family life frequently determine whether adults consult sexologists and sexopathologists.

The USSR Health Ministry issued a directive in May 1988 which has become a fundamental tenet regulating the activities of the country's sexological service. The new medical specialism of 'sexopathologist' has officially appeared for the first time.

Today, the prime link in the sexological service has to be the specialised unit of the medical-psychological consultation clinic organised on the basis of psychiatric (psychoneurological) institutions in cities of more than a quarter of a million people. The psychoneurological clinic is usually the base institution. The paramount functions of such clinics are therapy, diagnosis and treatment of sexual disharmony and disorders. There are several reasons for including these units in the psychoneurological service. First, according to many researchers, 70–90 per cent of the sexually sick have psychiatric disorders of a mainly neurotic type, while 50–60 per cent of patients have disorders which play a major part in their current sexual problems. Second, key mental disorders require differentiated methods of psychotherapy and psychopharmacology and ways of averting socially dangerous actions.

We now have new medical specialisms, like andrology and psychoendocrinology. How do such specialists interact and how do they share practical activity?

It is assumed that a sexopathologist should cover the whole spectrum of sexual disorders within the framework of partnership functions, that an andrologist is a specialist in problems of male infertility, and that a psycho-endocrinologist carries out diagnosis and treatment of sexual 'perversions', transsexualism and chromosome anomalies.

The tasks of family medical-psychological consultation units are:

- consultative-diagnostic selection of patients needing observation and treatment in the unit;
- comprehensive therapy of patients with sexual disorders through psychotherapy, physiotherapy, reflex-therapy, pharmacotherapy and specialised procedures;
- psychological diagnosis and correction methods for family relationship disorders;
- hygiene-educative and psychotherapeutic work with the public and, first and foremost, with people just entering marriage and couples divorcing.

Professional Training

A medical psychologist ought to be on the staff of every medical-psychological family consultation unit, which should also have a sexopathology doctor, a nurse, a laboratory assistant and a medical orderly. However, local health agencies may increase the salary rates of sexopathology doctors and medical psychologists, depending on the requirements of the area. In large towns several medical-psychological family consultation units may be brought together into a single large centre with a corresponding increase in staff. While coming within the structure of a psychoneurological clinic, the unit may have access to somatic polyclinics or other medical institutions in the area.

In line with the directive mentioned above, a sexopathologist should be a doctor who has trained in psychiatry and sexopathology. The psychiatric training of sexopathology doctors is necessary because they will have to assess the patient's mental state and differentiate between the complicated psychopathological symptoms and syndromes, and their psychosomatic relationships. The training of doctors in sexopathology is the responsibility of the Central Medical Training Institute in Moscow, and the Leningrad and Kharkov medical training colleges.

The scheme for medical specialisation and training in medical sexology envisages the training at the Moscow Central Training Institute of heads of family medical-psychological consultation units and chief specialists in sexopathology for regions and cities; the training of psychotherapists, sexopathologists and medical psychologists at the Leningrad College; and initial specialisation for doctors (four-month courses) at the Kharkov College. In addition, the Department of Sexology at the Leningrad State Doctor Training College provides courses for medical psychologists who are to work in medical-psychological family consultation units.

The orientation of the Leningrad Department (headed by S.S. Libikh) is the study of sexual harmony and disharmony, a psychosomatic model of sexual disorders, and the elaboration of psychotherapeutic and other treatment methods. The Kharkov Department (headed by V.V. Krishtal) studies somatic causes of sexual disorders and works on diagnosis and treatment methods. Despite the protracted organisational period, there is no sexology department in Moscow, but a short lecture course exists within the psychotherapy department.

The Soviet sexological service is based on the principle of ambulatory assistance, preserving a normal living pattern, carrying on normal work and sexual activity. The need for hospitalisation arises only in cases of acute psychopathological disorder (where a patient will be placed in a neurosis unit or a daytime in-patient psychoneurological clinic), vascular insufficiency of the genitalia (admission to an angio-surgical unit), acute urological illness (a urological unit) and specific endocrinopathy (an endocrinological unit). In-patient treatment is normally followed by a period of ambulatory sexual readaptation by the partners.

Analysis of visits to sexological clinics reveals the following picture: the bulk (up to 70–75 per cent) of patients have sexual problems of a psychological (psychic) nature; as already noted, women's visits to a sexopathologist account for no more than 10 per cent of the total number of patients; and the proportion of patients who come because of distorted knowledge about sex is fairly high (up to 10–15 per cent). It is noteworthy that people attending for reasons of sexual disharmony form about the same percentage as those with specific sexual disorders. Quite frequently the patient (almost always male) comes to the sexopathologist because of someone else's problems, because of claims made by a partner, which more often reflect that person's own sexual problems.

In recent years there has been a marked increase in visits from people with deviant sexual behaviour. At the same time, such rare patients are often under extreme pressure and fear owing to formal criminal responsibility and moral condemnation from society.

Problems of the Sexology Service

The major problem is the insufficient number of professional sexo-pathologists. While the large cities may well provide a sexopathologi-cal consultation service, the remote regions often have nothing at all. Further, the service is not very well coordinated. The regional method of resolving problems, together with a somewhat primitive approach in places, naturally results in a certain chaos. The USSR Scientific Centre on Sexopathological Issues has lost its function as an organising nucleus; it is now no more than a nominal structure. Other objective difficulties include insufficient training for sexopathological doctors in psychology, psychotherapy and psychiatry, which is evi-dent in their underestimation of psychogenic factors and knowledge of personal sexual problems concerning genitalia blood supply, the state of the prostate gland, and so on. We are only now laying the foundations for postgraduate doctoral training, improvement and specialisation.

The current dissolution of social and economic relations is also reflected in the lack of a common sexological conception and shortcomings in the organisation of the entire service. Sexopatholo-gist doctors suffer a shortage of audiovisual aids and technical equipment (computers, video-recorders, tape-recorders and so on). We have a special need of scientific and specialist information from abroad in the form of books, periodicals, annotations, elaborations and methodology.

We see a solution to the problem to some degree in developing non-state forms of medical activity. The beginning of the 1990s saw extensive promotion of individual medical activity and group work. Numerous medical cooperatives and profit-making centres are increasingly advertising the services of sexopathologists. The devel-opment of that type of medical practice reflects the public's demand for it. While encouraging the emergence of non-state alternative medicine, however, we should recognise the need to raise the professional level of sexopathology doctors in medical cooperatives and private centres.

The USSR Sexological Association 'Health and Culture' was instituted in February 1991; it is a voluntary public organisation bringing together scholars, educationists and practitioners for interdisciplinary investigation of sexual behaviour, sex education and sex culture. The Association's principal concerns are:

- to create expert interdisciplinary guidance for determining the importance of various programmes (reviewing popular, artistic and educational literature on sexological themes, and elements of artistic work, particularly in film and video programmes);
- to elaborate research projects for assisting scientific groups in putting them into practice: activating research through holding competitions and rewarding the best work;
- to coordinate research in the various branches of sexology (organising scientific conferences, seminars and colloquia);
- to provide independent expertise on the results of research and on professional competence from specialists in sexology, and to check the administrative competence of acts that are passed and the effectiveness and adequacy of new medical diagnostic methods;
- to take part in working out new organisational forms of education for children and adolescents, and the general public, to participate in discovering preventive measures to combat sexually transmitted diseases (primarily AIDS), and to provide medical-psychological help to families;
- to arrange international cooperation in research and government measures, and to exchange experience with other countries;
- to train and improve personnel for work in sexology;
- to set up medical diagnostic and consultation centres, ventures, funds, clubs and societies of sex culture, to publish and distribute scientific and popular material, and to help form a healthy way of life for everyone;
- to ensure social protection of Association members, including their rights as authors, and to ensure their creative development and the professional improvement of all Association members.

The major structural subdivisions of the Association are the Secretariat headed by a General Secretary (S.S. Agarkov), an audit committee and honorary membership. The leading Soviet sexologists

(G.S. Vasilchenko, I.S. Kon, S.S. Libikh and A.M. Svyadoshch) have been elected honorary members of the Association.

At the present time, the sexological service is going through a period of active reorganisation, the development of new forms and structures, and the search for new research projects, which should provide a strong basis for the future.

References

1. G.S. Vasilchenko, 'Sexopatologiya', in *Bolshaya Meditsinskaya Entsiklopediya* (Moscow: 1984), vol. 23, p. 196.
2. I.S. Kon, 'Sexologiya', in *Bolshaya Meditsinskaya Entsiklopediya* (Moscow: 1984), vol. 23, p. 190.
3. I.R. Tarkhanov, 'K fiziologii polovovo apparata u lyagushki', *Russkaya meditsina*, 1885, nos 30–2, pp. 1–26.
4. A.A. Ukhtomsky, 'Dominanta kak rabochy printsip nervnykh tsentrov', *Russky fiziologichesky zhurnal*, 1923, nos 1–3, pp. 31–45.
5. V.M. Bekhterev, 'O polovykh izvrashcheniyakh, kak patologicheskikh sochetatelnykh refleksakh', *Obozrenie psikhiatrii, nevrologii i eksperimentalnoi psikhologii*, 1914, nos 7–9, 357–82.
6. V.M. Tarnovsky, *Polovaya zrelost, yeyo techenie, otkloneniya i bolezni* (St Petersburg: 1886).
7. L.Y. Yakobzon, *Polovoye bessilie* (Petrograd: 1915); *Polovaya kholodnost zhenshchin* (Leningrad: 1927); *Onanizm u muzhchin i zhenshchin* (Leningrad: 1928).
8. M.A. Chlenov, 'Polovaya perepis moskovskovo studenchestva', *Russky vrach*, 1907, nos 31–2, pp. 1072–1111.
9. I.A. Popov, *Materialy iz polovoi zhizni muzhchiny. Diss. kand*, (Moscow: 1969).
10. I.S. Kon, *Vvedenie v sexologiyu* (Moscow: 1988).
11. G.S. Vasilchenko (ed.), *Obshchaya sexopatologiya* (Moscow: 1977).
12. V.S. Vasilchenko (ed.), *Chastnaya sexopatologiya*, vols 1, 2 (Meditsina, 1983).
13. *Aktualnye voprosy sexopatologii. Sbornik trudov* (Moscow: 1967).
14. *Voprosy sexopatologii. Sbornik trudov* (Moscow: 1969).
15. *Problemy sovremennoi sexopatologii. Sbornik trudov* (Moscow: 1972).
16. A.M. Svyadoshch, *Zhenskaya sexopatologiya* (Moscow: 1974).
17. Tarnovsky, *Polovaya zrelost*.
18. S.I. Golod, *Stabilnost semi: sotsiologichesky i demografichesky aspekty* (Leningrad: 1984).
19. L.Y. Gozman, *Psikhologiya emotsialnykh otnosheniy* (Moscow: 1987).
20. D.N. Isayev and V.Y. Kagan, *Psikhogigiena pola u detei* (Leningrad: 1986).

Index

abortion:
   deaths due to, 1, 59, 60
   legalisation of, 2, 5, 45
   out-of-hospital, 5, 51
   self-induced, 5, 45, 50
abortion, *see also* contraception
abortion (induced abortion (IA)), 5,
   48–9, 58–60
   as principal birth control method,
     5–6, 30–1, 45–6, 54–8
   statistics, 5–6, 47–54, Fig. 2.1
Adam's Rib film, 74
AIDS, 1, 5, 33, 109–10
   campaign against, 6–7, 10, 33–4, 35,
     163
   and homosexuals, 95–6, 101, 104
All-Union Beauty Contest (1989), 126–9
All-Union Scientific Method Centre on
   Sexopathological Issues, 155
ARGO (Association for Equal Rights
   for Homosexuals), 109, 110
Argumenty i fakty paper, 8, 31, 96–7,
   107
Armenia, 100
art, 17–18, 19, 20–1, 24–5, 90
Article 121 of penal code, 8, 34, 91–3,
   98
Article 132, draft law, 8–9, 98–9
Assassin, The film, 76–7, 82, 85
Asthenic Syndrome, The film, 80

ballet, 21, 25
BBC 'Inside Story' programme, 130,
   131
beauty, concept of, 121, 122–3, 125, 130
beauty contests, 74, 116
   criticisms of, 130–1
   future role of, 132
   international links, 118–19
   problems of, 121
   promotion of, 119–20
   search for Miss USSR (1989), 126–9

'sovietisation' of, 122–5
   Western influences on, 117–21
Belorussia, 9, 29, 101, 117, 138
Berdyaev, N., 1, 21–2
Beria, Lavrenty, 3
birth control *see* abortion; contraception
birth rates, fertility rates, 31, 45, 47, 59,
   60
Blown Kiss film, 75–6, 85
'blues' *see* homosexuals
books, educational, 10, 11, 94, 96
Borisenko, K., 101
brothels, 3, 32
Burgasov, N., 33, 95
Burn, The film, violence in, 70–1

carnivals, 18
censorship, 2, 9, 25, 35–6
Centre for Gender Studies, 10
charities and trusts, 10–11, 34–5
children:
   and AIDS, 7, 34
   sexuality of, 23, 26–7, 96
   and venereal disease, 5, 33
children, *see also* sex education
church, Russian Orthodox, 2, 17, 89
Communist Party, 3, 25–6, 36, 37–8, 39
Comrade Stalin's Trip to Africa film, 79
conservatism, in Russian society, 4,
   36–7, 41, 124–5
contraception:
   all methods, 56–7, Table 2.4
   condoms, 5, 31, 33, 56–7
   ignorance of, 53–4, 55–6
   oral, 5, 31, 46, 54, 56
   shortage of, 5, 7, 30, 54
   use of, 54–8, Table 2.3
contraception, *see also* abortion
courts, homosexual cases in, 92–3
Criminal Code, and homosexuality,
   90–2, 98–9

168   *Sex and Russian Society*

history of, 9–10, 26–7, 152–6
and homosexuality, 94
professional training in, 155, 160–2
sexual desire, 145, 149
sexual disorders, 155, 159–60, 161–2
sexual minorities, 7–8, 34, 103, 109–10,
see also AIDS; homosexuals;
lesbians
Sexual Minority Association, 104–5
sexual relationships, types, 149–51
sexual revolution, 3–4, 28–9
sexual satisfaction, 32–3, 147–51, 157
sexual violence, 6, 29, 75–8, 84, 85, *see
also* rape
sexuality, 16–17, 21–2, 23, 26–7, 96,
152–3
Slav paganism, 16–17
socialist realism, 66–7
society:
moral collapse of, 73, 79
and pornography, 37–9
sodomy, laws against, 89–90, 91
Soviet Research Centre on
Sexopathology, 154
SPID-info, AIDS periodical, 7, 35,
96–7, 105
Stalin, Joseph, 5, 45, 66, 79
Stalinism *see* repression
state, and public morality, 41–2
suicide, 1
surveys, 22–3, 54–5
of students, 29, 135–8

Svyadoshch, A.M., 26, 156, 164

Tema, gay newspaper, 7, 105
theatrical art, 21, 25, 36
To Die for Love film, 73
Tragedy Rock-Style film, 68, 69

Ukraine, 8–9, 47, 101, 138, 155
urban-rural differences, 30, 45, 50,
136–8, 144, Table 6.1
Uzbekistan, 52, 100, 117

Vasilchenko, G.S., 26, 155–6, 164
venereal disease, 5, 33, 101, 163
video, and pornography, 36–7, 38
violence, 29–30, 70–1, 101–2

Western influence, 6, 18–19, 37–8,
116–21
'Wings' (formerly 'Neva Shores'),
110–11
women, 84, 149
and contraception, 54–5, 56, 57
in films, 68, 69, 73–5, 76–8, 80–3
sexopathology of, 156–7
women, *see also* abortion; beauty
contests

Yakutia, Vilyuis college survey, 138
youth culture in films, 65–8